CW00495328

A Few Deeds Short of a Hero

Robert Widders

Text copyright © 2009 Robert Widders

Dedicated

To my dear friend H.W.

To Donald and Ginny

And above all, to my sister, Pam; she's played the hand that life dealt her with courage, grace, and dignity.

I would also like to say a special thank you to Katie Gutierrez for her excellent editorial input.

Table of Contents

Contents

Part One: The Royal Navy

Chapter One

It was a typical nineteenth century Wirral pub. The brickwork was blackened by a century of smoke and pollution, and a faded sign swung over the door. Father left us outside.

"I'm just nipping in for a quick drink and I'll be out in a minute," he said.

I was ten years old. My sister, Pam, was five. We peered through the door every time someone walked in or out. Mother wouldn't have approved of this. But she was ill and in hospital, and we were staying with our grandparents in the Dingle.

At intervals, Father came to the door to check on us. He brought crisps and a soft drink. Later, he dragged a drinking buddy out and briefly introduced us. We didn't want the crisps, or the drink-sodden affection. We just wanted to go home.

By the time the pub closed, Father could hardly stand. Pam and I led him to the station to catch the underground train back to

Liverpool. At the ticket barrier, I fruitlessly searched his pockets for the return tickets. As I rifled around, humiliated, the ticket inspector's eyes filled with pity and he waved us through. A short train ride later, we emerged into the smoky bustle of Lime Street Station, but Father's inability to walk three steps in a straight line without falling finally attracted the attention of the police. He was arrested, and we were left waiting in a bare, dingy office.

Eventually, a policeman ushered us into the back of a police car. One of them radioed the station to check the address to which we should be taken.

"What's the address, son?" the other one asked, peering back around to look at me.

I looked at him blankly, unable to remember, feeling stupid. He glanced at his colleague, and his look said it all: *Like father, like son.*

Mother eventually went to a solicitor to start divorce proceedings, a more difficult process then than it is now. The solicitor instructed her to gather evidence of adultery, so we would take Father's letters and hold them over the spout of the kettle, using the steam to soften the glue that sealed the envelope. Mother's eyes flicked constantly towards the door whilst we quickly read them. Then we expertly resealed the envelopes before the glue dried. We became adept at intercepting mail and discreetly checking coat pockets. My little fingers would probe through soft pocket linings, turning up an odd coin and the occasional indiscreet note. It was fun for me, but not for my mother, who was well aware of the consequences of Father catching us...

Rows were common. Mother and I were both attuned to Father's mood and alcohol consumption. I was totally partisan. My mother was right, and my father was wrong; it was that simple. I know now that there are two sides to every story. I'd like to understand my father and see his point of view. But it's hard - very hard.

Following a drawn out and unpleasant struggle, Mother was finally granted a divorce. After this, Father would sometimes call around on a Saturday to take Pam and me out for the afternoon. A trip on the Mersey ferries to New Brighton was a favourite. We enjoyed the fairground, with ice creams and a ride on the donkeys. It's hard to recall, though, how many days out were happy ones and how many were ruined by alcohol. The bad experiences were probably a minority, but they're the ones that come back to me with chilling clarity.

One afternoon, he took me to the pictures. We went by bus to a cinema near Edgehill, where Johnny Weissmuller was playing in a Tarzan adventure. Once inside, he turned to me, saying, "Just wait here, I won't be long." I didn't mind this. I was an independent boy and quite happy on my own. Later, much later, a torch flashed and the cinema manager called my name, his voice booming from the back of the cinema. I can still see my drunken father being escorted to me as I stood up. He looked no guiltier then than he had when he'd left me. Waves of shame and humiliation flooded over me, and I ran outside. Finding a number 79 bus to Lee Park, I sat down quietly on the upper deck.

"You look like you've seen a ghost," a woman commented solicitously.

"I have," I replied, not knowing what the hell else to say. I hoped she'd just leave me alone. She did, but the ghost of that day never truly does; sometimes it comes back to me, resurrected by some chance occurrence like a shout in the flickering light of a cinema.

One day I came home from school to find Mum sat talking to two men. Her hands were clasped tightly in her lap, and her eyes looked moist and red-rimmed. "Just take your sister out for a walk for a while, please," she said. When we got back, she explained that the men were plainclothes policemen. They'd called to inform her that my father had been found dead at work. He'd had such a quantity of alcohol in his bloodstream that it killed him. The news had the dubious distinction of a report in the *News of the World*. The most significant effect, from my perspective, was that it earned me the next day off school, plus another day off to look after my sister when Mother attended the funeral. Despite all that had happened, she was deeply saddened by the news of his death. That was unlike me; I just took it in my stride. I didn't cry - I didn't grieve.

After my father died, Mother had to apply for National Assistance. We went to the office in Garston, to fill in forms and be interviewed. It was a soulless, bare chasm of a building, painted in depressing smoke-stained magnolia paint, and the bastards made her plead for every penny. It was just the system, the relics of the means test, and nothing personal. But I hated them; to me, it felt very personal. I also hated going down to the warehouse where, once a year, free school blazers were issued to Liverpool's poorest children.

School on Monday mornings was just as unpleasant. For as long as I could remember, anyone on a low income who received free school dinners was treated differently. Each child's name was called before he or she handed in dinner money. With amazing insensitivity, the teacher would insist on calling my name out, and I would have to shout out, "Free dinners!" It happened every week. Surely they could have done things differently.

Poverty also provided lighter moments, however. We often didn't have enough money to pay the weekly rent, so sometimes we'd hide when the rent man called. We'd crouch behind the settee when we heard him knocking next door, trying not to giggle. Liverpool rent collectors were used to such tactics. Ours would peer through the window to see if we really were out. To me, it was a game. To the rent man, it was an inconvenience, but he knew he'd get the rent eventually. To my mother, it was a breathing space whilst she juggled the finances of poverty for another week.

At fourteen, I decided to follow in my father's footsteps and join the Royal Navy. With this settled, I couldn’t see much point in going to school anymore. Most mornings, I would have my name entered on the form register at Gateacre Comprehensive School. Then I’d climb over the wall into Grange Lane with my mate Rollo. We spent hours wandering around Lee Park and Netherley Estate, getting up to the occasional mischief.

Netherley was built on the site of the Pre-Fabs. These little prefabricated single-storey chalet-style houses were hurriedly erected after the Second World War. They were homes for people bombed out by the German air force during the Blitz. In the 1960s, the mature tended gardens, tidy homes, and established communities were bulldozed. The residents were moved into a 'modern' estate alongside the supposed beneficiaries of a city centre slum clearance scheme. This new estate, Netherley, then eventually evolved into a bleak ghetto.

Lee Park was older than Netherley. It had fewer soulless blocks of flats, and more semi-detached houses with gardens. The notable exception to this was the row of eleven-storey tower blocks, built on the edge of the golf course. Named after former prime ministers, like Eden and Macmillan, they really did tower above the rest of the estate.

The golf course was a frequent target of our mischief. We'd hide in the bushes, running out and grabbing the odd ball that went wide before the golfer could get to it. As amusing as this was, the run up to Guy Fawkes Day was our favourite time. Rollo had two parents, one of whom was in employment, so he was rich, and could afford to buy fireworks. We liked to get rockets and take them up to the top floorof the flats, which overlooked the golf course. Then we would use a length of pipe as a rocket launcher and bombard the golf course clubhouse. We fired the rockets at extreme range, which meant that scoring a hit was unlikely. It also kept us out of reach of any irate golfers. But we were within touching-distance of the front doors of the flats, which opened on the long verandah that ran along the side of the building. Not surprisingly, some people weren't thrilled at having amateur artillery on their doorstep, and they made their feelings clear. Once, a huge burly docker chased after us waving his fists. "I'll fuckin' 'av you little bastards!" he shouted. Unlike the actual Royal Artillery regiment, we beat a hasty retreat.

Most of our activities weren't as stupid, though once we stole a bottle of wine from an off license. I had most of it, going home half drunk and then heading straight to bed. I'm not sure how much my mother knew. Perhaps she hoped that the Navy would straighten me out. If that was the case, she was right.

Chapter Two

In April of 1970, I said my goodbyes to Mother and Pam at home. She was predictably sad, in the way that most mothers would be while watching their children go off to join the Navy. My mate Rollo took the bus into the city with me. We said a casual stiff-upper-lip goodbye at Liverpool Lime Street. A few hours later, I arrived at the railwaystation in Ipswich. The platform was dotted with spotty fifteen-year-old recruits, eyes glittering with a mixture of excitement and trepidation. We grouped together and chatted till buses came to take us to HMS Ganges, the Royal Navy training establishment at Shotley Gate.

On arrival, a rating not much older than us gave us a few items of uniform, showed us where to sleep, and organised a hot meal. In the evening, a petty officer told us to form up in three ranks outside the barrack room. He spoke slowly - he clearly didn't expect too much from us at this stage. "Either wear the oilskin coat or fold it over your left arm." Then he shouted, "Left turn - by the left, quick march."

We marched across to the gymnasium in the main camp. The petty officer shouted, "Halt!" and the long, silent column of children shuffled to a stop outside the gym. "Right then, you're gonna watch a film," he said. This sounded good, and everyone seemed to cheer up.

Inside, canvas chairs were laid out cinema style. We sat waiting expectantly. I looked around, reading quotes from Kipling's poem "If," which formed a decorative frieze around the walls: "If you can keep your head when all about you/Are losing theirs and blaming it on you," and so on. The words leered down at me, and I had a bad feeling about the place. I'd hated sport at school and had managed to avoid it, but I suspected that doing that wouldn't be so easy here.

The film was *Yangtze Incident*, the true story of HMS Amethyst's daring escape from the clutches of the Chinese, whilst trapped on the Yangtze River. Whether it was shown to entertain us and divert feelings of homesickness or to motivate us, I'll never know. However, it worked brilliantly on all counts and I went to bed feeling content with life.

For the first month, we lived in the Annexe, where we were introduced to the art of being a sailor, or naval rating. The Annexe was a little camp within a camp, separated by a road from the rest of HMS Ganges. It had brick walls, painted a depressing cream colour, and long barrack rooms lined with rows of beds. Petty officers harried us from parade ground to lecture room and myriad other places. To add to the confusion, they harried us using the Navy's own language. Some of this seemed so obscure that they actually gave us a lecture in understanding it.

"Now lads," said a rotund PO who had a permanently jolly expression, "I'm going to ask you a question. What did you have at dinner yesterday?"

Easy question, I thought, keeping my hand still and my mouth closed. The boy next to me shouted out, "Steak and kidney puddin's, PO."

"Wrong answer, peabrain. You had *babies' heads,*" the PO said. We all dutifully laughed. But I thought about it. I suppose the round bowl-shaped, suet coated, steak and kidney puddings did look a bit that way.

The PO called out some more questions, but no one was going to get caught out this time. "Right," he said, "Food is called *scran*, rubbish is *gash,* and soap powder is called *dhobey dust*." He continued for a while, and then he finished with a question: "What are those things you were issued with - you wears 'em in bed?"

This seemed a safe one, and a few voices called out 'pyjamas.' "Wrong, peabrains," the PO laughed. "They'm called *brown hatter's overalls*." He paused, knowing someone would ask why. "Never mind why," he said, "but they don't wear 'em in the Fleet."

The lecture finished; he refused to be drawn in further. I understand now why they're so called, but in these politically correct times, I'll do as the PO did and leave it at that.

Kit issue was not the slapdash ritual that I'd expected based on watching too many daft war films on the television. _Stores accountants took great care seeing that everything fitted, especially items like caps and boots. Our instructors took equal care, ensuring we gave every item its correct naval title.

"Now, never ever let me hear you call that a hat," the P.O. said. "It's a cap. Got it?"

"Yes, PO," we all dutifully chorused.

Needless to say, there was always someone who would forget and ask something like, "Do we have to wear hats with sports rig, PO?" The PO would then fling his cap through the air like some strange maritime Frisbee.

Kit upkeep took a big portion of our scarce leisure time. I was issued with a wooden stencil of my name and initials, which, for some unaccountable reason, was called a *type*. Our divisional PO, a chubby communications yeoman, showed us how to mark every item of kit with our name in paint.

"Now, just you remember this: no name, no claim. So see that all yer kit is marked so no other bastard can pinch it," he said.

He patiently taught us to wash, iron, wear, and stow away our uniforms. Looking after kit took on dimensions that few of us could ever have envisaged. Fortunately, I picked it up with ease. We had lessons in how to *dhobey* (wash) clothing. Stood two to a sink in the laundry room, we scrubbed each item and then took it to the PO. If it passed inspection, the PO then allowed us to rinse the item in another sink, and then it was ready for hand wringing and drying.

Everyone could deal with dhobeying. The thing that scuppered many lads was the necessity to iron everything and then fold it to ship's book size. The ship's book was the *Naval Ratings Handbook*, which was roughly the size of a thin hardback novel. We used vast quantities of starch to fold and iron every item until it was the shape of the book, and then we stacked them spine outwards in a locker. (Our lockers were never allowed to be locked, so that our kit could be inspected at any time, and I, like most others, kept my locker incredibly neat and smart.)

Unfortunately, before anything could actually be worn, it had to be ironed again to remove a mass of razor-sharp misplaced creases. No doubt this would have a time management consultant howling with derision. But we were being prepared to look after and stow large amounts of kit in the cramped confines of a warship's messdeck, so perhaps it wasn't as daft as it sounds.

When we weren't ironing kit or cleaning the antiquated barracks, we learned parade drill. We initially drilled on the tarmac next to the accommodation blocks in the Annexe and, later, on the big parade ground overlooked by the mast in the main camp. I'd already learnt basic foot and rifle drill in the Sea Cadets when I was 13, so it wasn't totally new to me.

Drill instructors taught using instructions and commands contained in a manual. Everything was done in a logical and structured way. First, they taught us how to stand to attention, then how to turn left and right, then how to march, and so on. The difference between left and right seemed to escape some lads at first, probably due to nerves. The instructor shouted, "Move to the left in threes - *leeee-ft*, turn," drawing out the word ‘left,’ then delivering 'right' in a sharp emphatic bark. Forty bodies swivelled on the heel of the left foot and the ball of the right. Forty pairs of arms remained tucked into the sides of bodies, fingers clenched and thumbs facing forward along the seams of the trousers. Forty pairs of heels came together, and forty pairs of eyes faced forward, as we stood rigidly to attention, in a column of threes, ready to march off.

Well, that's almost what happened. The lad on the far right of the front rank of the squad had turned right. Then the instructor shouted, "Squad, by the left, quii...ck, march." Forty left legs shot forward, and forty right arms swung forward, parallel with the ground. The squad of thirty-nine marched off, whilst the remaining lad marched away - in the opposite direction. He made a smart but lonely progress across the parade ground. Eventually, he realised he was alone, turned around, and ran back, accompanied by howls of laughter from the rest of the squad.

On another occasion, a squad was drilling with rifles and fixed bayonets. A lad fainted and fell forward, bayoneting the boy stood to attention in front of him. But accidents like that were extremely rare, though when they occurred, they were, like everything else, greeted with amusement. I enjoyed drill, and I threw myself into it with gusto. Not everyone did, though. The instructors screamed and shouted, but it wasn't personal. For one lad, though, the drill and discipline proved too much, and he deserted after a few days. I don't know what happened to him. The Navy is tough on deserters, but how tough could it be on a fifteen-year-old?

The scope for leisure activities was limited. We were always busy, and we weren't allowed to leave the Annexe anyway. There was plenty to amuse us, though. To save money, a couple of boys decided to cut each other's hair. Having no idea of how to do it properly, they alternatively trimmed and snipped until both were left bald. This being a breach of Queen's Regulations, they were both put on a charge. Another group decided to have a Ouija board session. One of them foamed at the mouth, had a fit, and was carried off on a stretcher by the medics, never to be seen again (by us anyway).

After a month, we were judged fit to be let loose on the main camp. Although it was a large shore establishment built in 1905, to the Navy this was a ship in commission, otherwise known as a stone frigate. It even had a one hundred and sixty foot high mast, taken from HMS Cordelia, a nineteenth century sloop. We were encouraged by our instructors to climb this during our leisure time. The powers-that-be considered this character forming, though since I knew modern warships didn't have masts, yardarms, and sails, I struggled to see the point.

Some boys vied with each other to see who could climb the highest. Occasionally, someone would climb to the very top and sit precariously on the button. I was happy to stay on the upper yardarms and watch the traffic on the river, with the odd Thames sailing barge making a brave sight in its sailing rig. The mast was a happy place, an escape from petty restrictions and rules and rituals that sometimes made life tiresome.

Possibly the most tedious of these rituals was the frenzied build-up of cleaning and polishing that went on every week in preparation for the captain's rounds. This was a weekly inspection of the messes where we lived. We painted walls. We polished floors until they gleamed. We scrubbed the toilets to a degree of whiteness undreamed of by their manufacturers. We polished anything made of brass (brightwork) to a mirror-like perfection with Brasso, which, like everything else, had an alternative name, 'bluebell.'

The ongoing need to refine personal kit added to this orgy of cleaning. Everything, even socks, was folded and ironed to achieve perfectly square corners, until my kit assumed an almost geometric appearance. When the captain eventually walked around on a Saturday morning, we weren't allowed to be seen anywhere near the messdecks. The whole place looked like some immaculate but recently deserted town. I never got to see the great man's reaction to our efforts. Was he impressed? I hope so.

The thing that really pissed me off, though, was sport. The ethos seemed (to me) to imply that no warship would win a battle or be safely crewed unless its men revelled in team games like cricket or football.

I detested football, and I resented being forced to buy an expensive pair of football boots from my pay (twenty-seven shillings a day before stoppages). The greatest misery, though, was the gymnasium, staffed by physical training instructors, or PTIs. They thought their actions instilled discipline and teamwork through sport. I saw things differently.

My particular nemesis was vaulting over the wooden horse. I never mastered this vital war-winning skill, much to the annoyance and despair of the PTIs. My argument that we were unlikely to encounter such objects during any future naval conflict merely brought threats of retribution. But I was to be proven right. The

Cold War, Northern Ireland, the Cod War, and the Gulf War, and not a wooden horse in sight.

Everything in the gym was done *at the double* and *with a jump*. Before explaining the next activity, the PTI would shout, "With a jump - to attention - go." We would all do a silly little jump in the air and land again with feet together and hands open at the side.

It was in the gym of HMS Ganges that I first heard the old joke about PTIs.

Someone leaned over and whispered, "What three special skills do you need to become a PTI?"

"I don't know," I whispered back.

"The strength of a carthorse, the speed of a racehorse, and the brains of a fucking rocking horse," he replied.

The urge to share this with the PTIs at the start of the next lesson was tremendous. But a healthy desire to keep my head on its shoulders kept me quiet. Instead, I contented myself with mentally cursing Kipling, whose poem continued to mock me from high up above the wall bars.

Chapter Three

The messdecks were located off the Long Covered Way, a lengthy, roofed path that ran from the main camp down to the river. It wasn't unusual to see some unfortunate youth puffing and panting up and down this hill, carrying his mattress on his head as a punishment for some minor transgression of naval regulations. The messes, where we kept our kit and slept at night, formed a division, and each division commemorated a long-dead naval hero. My own was Hawke Division, named after a former First Lord of the Admiralty.

No doubt Admiral Hawke would have approved of the warlike spirit of many of his division, who busied themselves at night exchanging batteries of improvised missiles between messdecks. Things got out of hand one night, and broom handles flew through the air, shattering a window. Howls of laughter were interspersed with *sotto voce* calls for quiet. But it was too late; the noise had attracted the attention of the duty instructor, who restored discipline. I usually managed to sleep through these little contretemps, but the punishments reached everyone that night, and I joined the rest as they beat a path up and down the long, covered way.

My own martial enthusiasm was reserved for the FN 7.62mm self loading rifle, or SLR, as it was more commonly known. I enjoyed drilling on the parade ground with it. With bayonet fixed, it was almost as tall as me. I must have looked an incongruous sight, like a white version of some unfortunate African child soldier.

I was happiest when we went to the ranges for live firing at figure eleven targets, whose scowling Johnny Foreigner faces seemed to invite a few rounds of full metal jacket. The SLR's high velocity bullet gave it a satisfying kick, which I enjoyed, and I discovered a certain degree of talent, achieving respectably tight groups in the centre of the target.

When not actually firing, some of us stood in a trench in front of and below the targets. I held up a long wooden stick and pointed to the place on the target where the last round had hit, for the boy firing to adjust his rifle's sights. The bullets cracked over my head like angry hornets, and I tried to imagine what it must be like to be fired at. When you're fifteen, such things seem exciting.

Eventually the team games, the gymnasium, and some of the more petty rules and regulations wore thin. I was coming up to the three-month period when it would be possible to purchase my discharge for twenty pounds. I started saving my money. Then disaster struck: one of my shirts was stolen. This meant I would have to buy another one, leaving me short of the full amount. My best oppos sensibly declined to lend me the money to make up the potential shortfall, but salvation came in the guise of an unmarked shirt in the drying room. Seizing the opportunity, I took the shirt and paint-stamped my name inside the collar and sewed a nametag above the pocket.

Unfortunately, the rightful owner discovered who had half hitched his shirt. He had two options: fight me for it or take the matter up officially. He chose the latter.

Things started out badly for me. I was sat on my bed dressed in pyjamas when another boy came, saying I was wanted in the Divisional Office. He convinced me that it would be all right to go dressed as I was. Of course, he was having me on, and when I walked into the office, the duty PO exploded.

"What the fuck do you think you're doing, coming in here dressed in brown hatter's overalls?" he said.

Realising I had been conned, I hurriedly went off to change, vowing dire revenge on the messenger. I returned to the office with the shirt, which I'd been told to bring back with me. The rightful owner was also stood there.

"Give me the sodding shirt," snapped the PO. He looked at it, read my name, and then flung it back to me.

"No name, no claim," he said to the other boy.

A few days later, I received a message to report to the Regulating Office. The regulating staff is the Navy's police, and a summons there surely meant trouble. Feeling anxious, I reported as ordered.

The regulating petty officer smiled at me sympathetically. “Doesn’t your mother love you any more, young Widders?”

I stared at him in bewilderment, and he explained that having written to inform her of my forthcoming discharge, the letter had returned stamped ‘not at this address.’ They then discovered that she’d moved to Devon to live with my grandmother. I don’t know what surprised me the most, my mother’s move or the discovery that the regulating staff was actually human.

My Gran had invited Mother to come and live with her. But moving to Devon was a tremendous task for my mother. She carried her own belongings in a suitcase, plus my sister's clothes and toys in a shopping bag. She and my sister went by bus to Liverpool Lime Street railway station and took the train to Newton Abbot. She told me all about it after I left HMS Ganges and arrived on her doorstep. I remember being annoyed when I discovered that she had thrown away my teddy bear. But she'd had to abandon virtually everything she owned. She did it to be closer to her own mother, wanting somehow to make up for lost time; she had been given to a children's home as a child. But she lost the strong bonds of friendship and solidarity typical of Liverpool, something she later deeply regretted.

My discharge from the Navy came as a surprise to my mother and a shock to my Gran. She wasn’t thrilled at having a teenage boy come to live with her, and who can blame her. Work was easy to find. I went to the Labour Exchange, and they sent me for a job in Halfords, in Queen Street, Newton Abbot. The work was pleasant but boring. My pay was five pounds a week, of which three went toward my keep and one toward repayments for the civilian clothes Mother had bought on credit for me. This left me with one pound a week, which wasn’t much, even then. In fact, I’d had almost as much disposable income during my last year at school, when I’d earned fifteen shillings a week from doing two paper rounds. So, full of the restlessness that’s dogged me throughout life, I decided that filling shelves was not for me.

Three months later, I went down to the Navy recruiting office in Plymouth, and they said they would be happy to take me back. The process was straightforward, especially the medical. I went to the Medical Officer's room, and the doctor looked up and said, "Hello, Robert." It was Dr. Evans, my old GP from Liverpool. His marriage had broken up, and he'd decided to join the Navy himself. The medical was nothing more than a quick signature on some papers and an enquiry about my mother's health.

Shortly afterward, I arrived at Plymouth railway station carrying my pusser's grip (holdall), with my old HMS Ganges cap slung on the handle. Full of confidence, I spotted the rating collecting recruits for HMS Raleigh, and I went up to him and asked for transport. He cast an eye over me and said, "Piss off, this transport is for recruits." When I finally convinced him that I was a recruit, I joined the others on the bus and was driven through Plymouth and across the Tamar on the Torpoint ferry to Cornwall.

Chapter Four

HMS Raleigh was the new entry training camp for adults, aged sixteen plus. Although I was still fifteen, I was now too old to go back to HMS Ganges for a full year. Raleigh was a mass of World War I vintage wooden accommodation huts, spreading out around three sides of a parade ground; the fourth side held various administrative buildings.

Compared to Ganges, life at Raleigh was a doddle. Most of the recruits were a fair bit older than me, though it didn't stop them struggling with kit and discipline sometimes. But my previous three months at Ganges had been the perfect preparation, and it made recruit training at Raleigh seem easy. Even the gymnasium was tame by comparison. The PTIs didn’t seem quite so badly obsessed by wooden horses, and there were cross-country runs and an easy assault course to bring variety. After the first few weeks, we were allowed shore leave. A favourite activity was a trip to the launderette in Torpoint. Whilst the washing was in the machines, we'd go to the pub next door and have a pint.

Once, whilst a crowd of us were sat there drinking, the door opened and a policeman walked in. Despite Raleigh being an adult training camp, some of us were well under the legal drinking age, and there was a sudden exodus of uniformed bodies in the direction of what we fondly imagined was the rear exit but was actually an enclosed yard. The bobby obviously had better things to do, and after a while it was obvious that nothing was going to happen. So we all sidled back in, trying to look casual and ignoring the jeers and caustic comments thrown at us.

Raleigh was a melting pot of different ages and social backgrounds, with people from every part of the country. I was Liverpudlian, uneducated, and very working class. Some of my shipmates amazed me. One Saturday afternoon, whilst on shore leave with a mate, I suggested getting a hamburger from a stall next to the cinema.

My Liverpool accent was thick enough to cut with a knife. “Ay, d’yer fancy an amberger, den?” I said.

We bought them, and as I stepped off in the direction of Union Street, my friend said in faultless English, “I couldn’t possibly walk along the street whilst I’m eating.”

He was horrified at the thought of it. But there were probably lots of things that he’d never experienced, such as the desperation that comes when your only pair of shoes is stolen. The marvellous thing about the armed services, though, is that they are a great social leveller. It doesn’t matter what you had or didn’t have before you joined. Everyone is in the same boat, struggling to make their way through a new society with its own culture, language, dress codes, and customs.

One day, an instructor appeared with a box. We recognised the contents immediately. "This," the instructor said wearily, "is the new S6 Respirator."

"Looks like a gas mask to me, Chief," one rating said. "Me Granny had one durin' the war. She told me all aboot it."

"Shut your stupid fuckin' Geordie gob!" the instructor shouted. Spittle flew from his mouth, his face went red, and he waved the goggly alien eyes of the respirator at us. "It's an anti-gas respirator - proof against biological agents, as well as nerve gas and other lethal agents that can be inhaled."

As part of the training in their use, and to give us confidence in their efficiency, our instructors marched us off to a building where we sat in a large room wearing our respirators, whilst CS gas was released from canisters burning in the corner. CS smoke, as it is properly called, is the stuff that was used for riot control. It isn't lethal, but in a confined space, it lives up to its incapacitant designation.

"You'll only ever have to do this once in your service career," the instructor lied in a muffled voice through his respirator. Then, one by one, we removed our respirators and stood in the choking smoke to shout out name, rank, and number before walking outside. I stood in the fresh air, my eyes burning, and gasped for breath. *Fine*, I thought, mentally cursing the instructor. *The sodding thing works, but I'd have been happy to take your word for it!*

When basic training finished, the Navy awarded me the prize for best recruit. As usual, they marked the occasion with a ceremonial passing out parade. Our class formed the guard of honour for the visiting dignitary. Being part of the guard, I was dressed in No1 uniform with white belt and gaiters, and carrying a rifle with fixed bayonet. The visiting admiral inspected the parade and then took the salute as we led the march past the dais where he stood with the captain.

The British forces do these things well. I felt full of pride and élan, as we marched to the sound of the Royal Marine band beating out "Hearts of Oak." With the inspection and march complete, the parade returned to its original position. We were stood at ease and I was called forward. Crashing to attention, I marched smartly forward to stand in front of the visiting officer, Admiral Sir

Horace Law, who had served at sea throughout the Second World War and was a descendent of Lord Nelson's elder brother, William Nelson. We exchanged salutes, and he presented me with a bosun's call, or naval whistle, engraved with the date and my name.

"What do you want to do with your career?" he asked.

My mind went blank as I stared at his uniform festooned with medal ribbons and gold braid. Realising that I was too overawed to speak, my divisional officer replied on my behalf, "He wants to be a mechanician."

I had no idea what a mechanician was, but everyone seemed satisfied with this, and I was sent back to take my place in the guard. Then the parade finished, and we marched back to our billets. It felt marvellous to be finished with basic training, a recruit no longer.

Chapter Five

After basic training,we all said our goodbyes and went off to various training ships for trade training. I was drafted to HMS Cambridge, a gunnery school and firing range perched on the cliffs at Wembury near Plymouth. The accommodation was in relatively modern 1960s-looking brick buildings. Plain eight-man rooms held a bed and a big wooden wardrobe/locker for each person. There was even a golf course along the edge of the camp, though it was wasted on me.

The 20mm Oerlikon guns, 40mm Bofors guns, and various types of big twin 4.5-inch gun turrets all faced out to sea. We learnt how to load and fire them at floating targets towed by boats from RAF Mountbatten, the Air Sea Rescue base nearby. Then we fired shells with proximity fuses at long, red fabric sleeve targets towed behind Hawker Hunter jet fighters. Because proximity fuses explode within a certain range of the target, we could never actually directly hit it. But it was all great fun in a boys' own comic sort of way. I didn't realise just how outdated and even obsolescent some of our weaponry was. The Oerlikon and Bofors were tried and tested technology during and before the Second World War, but we were facing modern Soviet jets. Nonetheless, I thought we were the cutting edge of naval warfare, and eagerly looked forward to joining the fleet as a gunner on a warship.

My weekends were free, unless I was on duty watch. I used to go home on Sundays to visit my mother in Newton Abbot. Mother was still living with Gran, and she would cook a big Sunday roast. I'd go up to the Bell Inn in Kingsteignton first for a few pints before lunch. After lunch I'd invariably fall asleep on the settee.

Mother was unhappy living with Gran. She realised that she couldn't make up for the lost years before the war, when she'd been put into a children's home. And Gran had got used to living alone and liked to have things done her way. So Mother applied to the council for housing, and eventually she got a rented house a few doors away in Margaret Road. Her finances were still precarious. I had made an allotment of ten shillings a week to her, deducted from my pay and paid directly by the Navy. It wasn't much, about half a day's pay (as a junior seaman) after stoppages. But the dole office threatened to stop her money if the allotment continued. So I quietly gave her some cash now and then instead, though she was always loath to accept it.

Being a junior seaman, I had to be back by 23:59 on Sunday night. One Sunday, I booked a taxi to take me from my home to the railway station, and it never turned up. Desperate to get back on time, I grabbed my suitcase and sprinted the mile and a half to the station. Predictably, I missed my train, and when I eventually arrived back on board, I was five minutes late. *Not too bad under the circumstance*, I thought. Not good enough, thought the Navy, and I was put on a charge. Some days later, my name appeared on a list of defaulters to be seen by the commander.

I was marched in: "Left right, left right, left right, left, defaulter 'shun,' left turn, off caps." The Master At Arms took a breather from his shouting and looked at me suspiciously, whilst I stood rigidly to attention in front of the commander's table. The charge was read out, something to the effect that on so-and-so date, I was charged with returning from weekend leave five minutes adrift (late). Given the option of pleading innocent or guilty, I chose the latter and was allowed to explain my extenuating circumstances. All seemed to be going well - the commander even looked sympathetic - when my divisional officer jumped in.

"Nonsense, he could easily have got a bus instead. I know, because I used to live in Newton Abbot myself," he said.

He may well have once lived in Newton Abbot, but it didn't mean there was a bus available when I'd needed one. I didn't have the wit to argue the point, though, and I was still too young to have the confidence to stand up for myself in what felt, at the time, to be an intimidating atmosphere. So I was awarded two days' stoppage of leave and a fine of a day's pay. All due to my divisional officer - and the ironic thing was that he was supposed to be there speaking on my behalf.

One evening, when I was part of the duty watch, I was sent out as bowman in a small boat to bring in a dinghy that was moored toa buoy in the bay. We had to bring it in because the weather was getting rough. The coxswain took us close to the buoy. He shouted to make himself heard against the noise of the wind, "Untie that boat from the buoy, and make the line fast to the side!"

I tied the dinghy alongside us, and we headed in the direction of the jetty. Then the engine cut out. The coxswain fiddled with the engine, and I turned round to help. But we couldn't restart it. "What now, 'swain?" I asked, spluttering through a face full of windswept spray.

He laughed. "Fuck all we can do, Scouse!" The incoming tide was sweeping us towards the shore. Eventually, the boats crashed up on the rocks. We both jumped out, clambering through the rocks and seaweed onto the beach. The duty watch waded into the water and started dragging the boats ashore before they were totally destroyed, and the coxswain and I were sent to get dry clothes and a welcome cup of tea.

I never thought any more about it, but the coxswain must have put in a good word for me. A few days later, I was called to the regulating office and told they were going to waive the rules and send me on weekend leave before my flight abroad the following week to join my first ship.

After the weekend off, I was sent to RAF Brize Norton for a flight to Malta, to await the arrival of my ship, HMS Grenville. I'd never been abroad before, so it was all a great adventure. On the plane, a flight attendant announced that we would be stopping to refuel in Cyprus and that passengers for Akrotiri should disembark and take the first bus and passengers for Luqa should take the second bus. These were the Cypriot and Maltese airfields, but I didn't have a clue what they were talking about. Not wanting to look ignorant, I took a guess and boarded the Akrotiri bus. I would have missed my ongoing flight but for the RAF driver, who shouted out an explanation on the bus. I scrambled sheepishly off again, giving everyone else a good laugh.

After arriving in Malta, I was taken to HMS St. Angelo, a huge fort, which was originally the headquarters of the Knights of

Malta. They had taken it over in 1530 and defended the island against the Turks, and then the Royal Navy moved in during the early twentieth century. My ship wasn't due in for a few days, so I was put to work under the supervision of a Maltese leading seaman who was in charge of keeping the place clean. There were two other ratings there who were also waiting for the HMS Grenville, and we quickly teamed up. The Maltese killick knew he wouldn't have much success in getting us to work, so he left us to our own devices. Nominally, we started work at about 0600 hours and then finished at lunchtime, before it became really hot. This left the rest of the day to us, and we could go ashore or spend our time in the little bar next to the accommodation block inside the fort. Though the currency had recently been decimalised in Britain, they were still using pounds, shillings, and pence in Malta. A bottle of Hop Leaf, the local beer, cost sixpence in the camp bar. This was amazingly good value, and we took full advantage of it.

One of the older lads took me to see the local sights. We visited all the bars in the gut, a long narrow alley that ran through Valetta. These bars had been the haunts of British sailors for generations, and their walls were covered with ships' crests. There were names like Rodney and Repulse, and many others less well-known. It was fascinating to read through them; like an informal roll of honour, it brought home to me just how big the Royal Navy had once been.

It was also interesting to look at the ladies of dubious virtue who also lined the walls of some of the bars. They were extremely good at separating Jack from his money. A favourite trick was to sit on a sailor’s knee and ask him to buy her a drink, which would then be brought over by the barman, who was in on the scam. When it was time to leave, the unfortunate sailor would be charged ten shillings for champagne, when he thought he had been buying lemonade, which of course it was. I never fell for this sort of thing, nor did I succumb to the temptation to purchase any more intimate favours, but it was certainly an education that most boys just past their sixteenth birthday don’t get.

One morning, I was sent for and told that HMS Grenville had just tied up alongside the jetty next to the fort. It was thrilling to finally join my first seagoing ship. There was also a touch of trepidation when, later that morning, I went through one of the fort's gates carrying my kit down to the jetty. The sight that greeted me has stayed etched in my mind to this day. Blazing sunlight reflected the blue Mediterranean waters in dappled patches against the grey paint of HMS Grenville's long, rakish hull. To a more knowledgeable eye, her minimal armament and old-fashioned funnel and masts betrayed her age. But she looked awesome to me as I walked up the brow and saluted the quarterdeck.

Upon the ship, my first task was to complete a joining routine. Essentially, this was a list of departments that had to be visited to have extra kit issued, pay and administrative details recorded, and so on. Later in my career, I learnt how to make this last a couple of days in barracks, but back then, I swiftly got on with it and started work.

HMS Grenville was a Type 15 anti-submarine frigate, with AS10 anti-submarine mortars, plus sonar that I learnt little about except that it really did go *ping*. Guns were my department, but, disappointingly, she only had one of them, a Mk 5 twin-barrelled 40mm Bofors, mounted on an open turret just abaft the bridge. She was launched in 1942 as a U class destroyer and then converted to an anti-submarine frigate in 1954, when she lost most of her armament and had an extra deck added.

Being on an old ship had its advantages. The crews of modern warships slept in bunks, but HMS Grenville was one of the oldest ships still in commission, and some of the crew still slept in hammocks. Like many things in the Navy, this was decided by seniority, and as the most junior person in the junior seamen's messdeck, I was given a hammock. Unlike a bunk, where the mattress and bedding were quickly and easily zipped up inside a cover, a hammock had to be slung before getting into it, then lashed up, taken down and stowed away in the morning. This was inconvenient, but something that I quickly became used to. At sea in rough weather, a hammock really proved its worth. When others pitched about from side to side on their bunks as the ship rolled, I was cocooned in my hammock, which swung naturally with the motion.

All the junior seamen lived together in one messdeck, with an easygoing leading seaman called Roger, who was the killick of the mess. We had another killick in there, a leading regulator called Trevor, who, despite being ship's policeman, was decent enough, too. Our mess was situated next to the galley and above the boiler room, so we didn't have far to carry meals, which were collected from the galley and eaten in the mess.

At sea, the heat from the boiler room warmed the messdeck nicely, though it attracted cockroaches. All old ships have their share of these repulsive little creatures, but the combined attractions of heat from the boiler room and food from the galley made our messdeck the *des res* that all cockys aspired to. During the day, they hid away in the mass of pipes, electrical wiring, and ventilator trunking on the bulkheads and deckhead. At night it was a different story. If you shined a torch on the locker where we kept the tea and sugar for brewing up, dozens and dozens of cockys would scurry away from the beam. They even found their way inside kit lockers, and it wasn't unusual to shake a cocky or two out of my clothes when I took them out of my locker. We sprayed various toxic bug killers around, but the cockroaches always reappeared, and everyone just learned to live with it.

The ship spent the next couple of weeks involved in various naval exercises. We would go to sea for a day or two, and then come back and moor to a buoy in the Grand Harbour or Sliema. All the seamen had a particular part of ship to work on daily. My part of ship was the starboard waist, where the whaler was slung on davits that could be turned out to lower it over the side. We would muster every mooring at 0800, under a PO who was nicknamed Slim, because he wasn't. Along with a few ordinary and able seamen, I scrubbed decks and bulkheads, polished brass scuttles (portholes) and chipped paint, and then repainted whatever we had just chipped paint off of. This happened every day, whether in sea or in harbour.

There were also watchkeeping duties at sea. The nautical day is divided into four-hour watches, except for the first dog (watch) at

1600, which lasts for two hours and the last dog at 1800, which also lasts for two hours. The first watch starts at 2000, the middle watch starts at 2359, the morning watch at 0400, the forenoon watch at 0800, and the afternoon watch at 1200.

The seamen were divided into four groups, the 1st and 2nd of both port and starboard, which, to confuse matters, were also called watches. These watches each worked a watch of one in four. For example, if the 2nd of port worked the forenoon, they would then work the first, followed by the afternoon watch and so on. Because the dog watches only last two hours, the watches rotate over a period of days, so everyone gets a fair share of the unsociable hours.

Confused? Well, I certainly was, for the first few days, until I got the hang of it. The best watch, which came once every four days, was the last dog followed by all night in bed - unless you were unlucky and some evolution was scheduled, which might call for the involvement of everybody whether nominally off watch or not. The worst watch was the middle. By the time you finished at 0400, there were only a couple of hours to sleep before call the hands. Then it was time to get up for a wash and shave followed by breakfast, where you had to be ready to start the day's work.

A typical morning watch would go something like this: At 0345, a hand shakes my hammock, and a low voice trying not to disturb the rest of the mess whispers, "Wakey, wakey, Scouse, time to go on watch." I grab the metal bar attached to the deckhead a foot or so above my face, hoisting myself out of my hammock and landing on the floor, silently cursing whilst reaching to my locker for No8 working rig and steaming boots. I put on my foulweather jacket, plus seaman's knife and marlin spike, which gets slung around my waist in a holster like a cowboy's gun belt. Then I make my way up to the upper deck, via a diversion to the for'ard heads for a piss.

Up on deck, the killick, or leading seaman, of the watch is detailing the hands for their various duties. Someone has already been sent to the wheelhouse, and someone else has just been detailed for bridge messenger. That's a shame, because I like that job. It's warm and dry on the bridge, and there's always something going on to make it interesting.

“Does anyone fancy being lifebuoy ghost?” the killick asks.

“I’ll do it, hookey,” I say, fancying a quiet hour on the quarterdeck with nothing to do but keep a lookout astern and alert the bridge should someone happen to fall overboard. Wandering down to the quarterdeck, I find the lifebuoy sentry, as he is more properly called, and take over. It's 0400 exactly, but my predecessor isn’t wasting time with congratulations for good timekeeping; he’s off to get his head down.

It’s a beautiful warm moonlit night with a calm sea; some people pay a lot of money for a Mediterranean cruise, but I’m getting paid to do it. An hour later and boredom has set in. I think about friends and family back home, wondering if my father sailed these same waters and stood gazing over the quarterdeck. Did he dream about meeting a girl and getting married? Could he have imagined that, one day, a son would follow in his footsteps? But enough introspection. Perhaps someone will oblige me with a little excitement by falling overboard, but no one ever does. Then my relief appears, and I join up with the rest of the watch on deck.

We sit around chatting and have a quick cup of tea. Then at 0540, it's my turn to go up to the bridge as starboard lookout. The lookout hands me the binoculars and points out a couple of lights in the distance at green (starboard) two zero and green two five. He's off to report to the officer of the watch; I can hear his voice reciting the time-honoured report, "Starboard lookout relieved, sir, all objects in sight reported, starboard navigation light and masthead steaming light burning brightly."

For the next twenty minutes I scan the horizon in vain. There's nothing new to report. My relief appears, and it's my turn to report to the officer of the watch. Then back to the starboard waist, just in time to help the rest of the watch carry sacks of potatoes down from the upper deck spud locker to the galley. It's not our job, but the killick of the watch has done a deal with the cooks, and in return we get hot bacon sandwiches and a mug of tea. Suitably fortified, it's back to the quarterdeck for another hour of lifebuoy ghost. I'm getting a bit tired now. I'll have to be careful; last night during the middle watch, I was so tired I nodded off for a second and tripped over a bollard. I try singing to keep myself awake, and the voice of the PO of the watch calls out good-humouredly, "Pipe down, you noisy bastard." *Where did he spring from*? I wonder, and shout back a suitable reply.

It's 0700 and my relief appears. "Good news, Scouse, the officer of the watch has stood down the lookouts," he says. I'm glad now that I didn't end up down in the wheelhouse or on the bridge as messenger. With no more lookout duties, the rest of the watch can enjoy more tea whilst sitting on the warm deck next to the funnel. Then 0800 comes and we have an hour off for breakfast and a wash and shave before starting the day's work at 0900.

Malta was a great place, and I was sorry to leave it behind when we set sail for England. As we headed west, the balmy Mediterranean showed its true colours, and we had twenty-four hours of gales so bad that it wasn't safe to work on the upper deck. Then, just as quickly as it started, the weather changed to brilliant sunlight, with seas so calm and clear you could see the gills on the huge basking sharks that patrol the sea. On our port side, the Atlas

Mountains brooded over the North African coast, and I stared avidly through binoculars and promised myself that I'd travel there one day.

When we arrived in Gibraltar, I was disappointed to find that we were only going to be there for one night and that my watch was on duty. Yes, we had duty watches in harbour, too; twenty-four hours doing different tasks, such as manning the gangway and fire and emergency duties. So I missed Gib this time, though I was to return to it many times in the future.

The next day, we set sail for the final leg of our journey back to England. For most of my colleagues, it was a routine trip, but for me it was part of a steep learning curve. I was the butt of good-humoured nautical practical jokes, of the 'go and collect a bucket of superheated steam from the engine room' variety.

One day one of the lads asked me if I'd seen the periscope. *I'm not going to fall for that one*, I thought. "Only submarines have periscopes, so bugger off," I said. He persisted, though, and lifted a cylindrical metal cover off what was obviously some sort of optical device. Then he took me down to the operations room, and lo and behold, there was a periscope for the officer of the watch to look through when the ship was totally closed down (sealed up) for operating in a contaminated nuclear environment.

He told me about the pre-wetting system, as well, which was fitted to wash nuclear fallout or chemical weapons off the upper deck. It was an amazing assemblage, which I would later see in use. The upper deck had a system of pipes like an upside down fire sprinkler that pumped vast quantities of sea water into the air, so the ship sailed along in a torrent of its own manmade rain.

Back in England, we berthed in Portsmouth dockyard, a place that I was to see a lot of during the next couple of years, despite the fact that we were a Devonport-based ship. Our anti-submarine role was nominal, too, with most of our time spent taking trainee officers to sea, or trying out new equipment before it was introduced to the fleet. Eventually, HMS Grenville went into dock and the anti-submarine mortars were removed and a modern mast fitted to replace the old lattice one. Big white domes were fitted on this mast for a new navigation system, code-named Abbey Hill. Satellite navigation is common enough now, but at the time it was all hush-hush and we weren't allowed anywhere near the thing.

Being a curious youth, I usually managed to have a look at any new kit. However, on one occasion even my wiles failed. A helicopter landed a large cased object on the quarterdeck and then flew off. The whole of the upper deck, aft of the bridge, was put out of bounds, and we were told in no uncertain terms to keep away and keep quiet about it. A while later, another helicopter flew in, lifted it off, and took it away. The general consensus of opinion was that we had been the staging post for the transportation of a nuclear bomb.

Our role as a trials ship also meant we were available to do some of the odd jobs that the Navy was asked to do. Once we took someone's cremated ashes and scattered them out at sea. On another occasion we sailed with the coffin of a dead sailor laid out on the quarterdeck for burial at sea. There were square shapes cut out of the side to stop it from floating; I'd never seen a corpse before, and I peered through, trying to see who was inside. An indistinct white shrouded shape lay there, ready for its watery grave. My curiosity satisfied, I cleared off below for a cup of tea. When I came back a bit later, the coffin was gone.

Life was interesting, though there wasn't the degree of exotic foreign travel that I'd expected. We did visit some European ports, including Den Helder and Rotterdam. Once, we visited France to represent Great Britain in some VE day anniversary celebrations. Regrettably, I can't remember exactly where and when. I think we sailed down the Seine to Rouen, where we enjoyed tremendous hospitality from the French. The ship was open to visitors. Lots of French ladies arrived, and we did all we could to firmly cement the *entente cordiale.*

But the part of the visit that will always stand out in my mind was the trip to the Pernod distillery. Brewery visits are a common and appreciated part of most visits to foreign ports. The usual routine is a tour around whatever brewery, followed by a few wets in their canteen. I never knew any sailor who was genuinely curious about brewing and distilling, but everyone feigns a degree of interest in return for a pleasant afternoon away from work and a couple of free drinks.

But not this time. We were taken straight to their bar, and someone welcomed us with the words, "We won't show you around, please just stay here and drink as much as you want." I don't think they envisaged the eventual outcome. When we finally left, most sailors staggered and swayed, some almost crawled, and a couple were carried. No one walked perfectly upright, including me. I don't know if anyone ever thanked the Pernod distillery for its generosity. But if anyone involved should ever read this, you have our heartfelt gratitude.

Back in England, during the early 1970s, the IRA was beginning to make its presence felt, and that had some unexpected effects upon us. Whenever we went ashore, with the exception of Portsmouth and Plymouth, we had to wear full No1 uniform. This is the traditional bell bottomed trousers and blue collar. Whilst the lads used to whinge about not being allowed to wear civvies, in reality many of them used to like to wear uniform. I certainly did. When the ship visited places like Gateshead and Newcastle, we'd have a tremendous time. People would buy us drinks in pubs, and the girls certainly showed their interest. The security situation changed this, though, and wearing uniform was made optional.

The regulations about civvies were, I felt, worse than wearing uniform. Jeans and tee shirts were not allowed, and we had to wear proper trousers, collar and tie, and a jacket. These regulations gradually eased over the years, but I still often used to wear my uniform to hitchhike home on leave, as it guaranteed getting a lift and saving money on rail fares.

Chapter Six

I took my first step on the dizzy road to promotion and was rated up from Seaman Gunner basic to Seaman Gunner 3rd class. Then, at the age of seventeen and a half, I was rated Ordinary Seaman. The practical implication of this, apart from a small increase in pay, was that I left my hammock behind and took over the mixed blessing of a bunk in the aft seamen's messdeck. Six months later, I was rated Able Seaman (AB) at the age of eighteen. Two things happened then. My pay increased again, which was welcome, but the Navy also started counting my modest efforts as a sailor as time served.

For reasons that remain a mystery—to me at least—service before the age of eighteen didn't count against the engagement for which you had signed on. Despite having served nearly three years already, my nine-year contract was only just starting. So now I was an AB, with a couple of year's sea time and a tattoo. (The tattoo was an off-the-wall crossed flag design done at the tattoo shop in the

Arches along the Hard in Portsmouth. I'd sat there looking insouciant, pretending that it didn't hurt, though it bloody well did.)

There was always something new to make life interesting. Once, when we were sailing down the English Channel during a storm, we were diverted to answer a distress call. A merchant coaster was adrift without power, and we were tasked to take it in tow. I was on the morning watch. The sky was beginning to lighten in the east. It was quite beautiful, with dark, threatening storm clouds and huge green wind-flecked waves. The buffer (chief boatswain's mate) appeared and shouted at three of us sheltering in the lee of the funnel. "Never mind gapin' at the fuckin' sky—get down to the stern an' lay out the towing hawser!" The seas were coming over the stern, onto the quarterdeck. To my surprise, the other two lads were clearly reluctant to go down on to it.

The Buffer led by example and started doing the job himself. He seemed incredibly old to me then, though I expect he was only in his mid-forties. I couldn't let the old boy struggle by himself, so I lent a hand and we flaked the hawser out on deck. By now the other part of the watch had been called, and we had enough hands to finish the job and prepare a gun line to be fired at the other ship, which was coming into sight.

A lieutenant appeared and took charge. The gun line, fired from a specially adapted rifle, was attached to another larger rope, which would be hauled across and then used to haul the towing hawser over. The other crew caught the gun line, but it broke under the strain.

We needed to get close enough to pass a stronger rope, which could be thrown by hand. The captain had the tricky job of bringing the ship stern on (backwards) to the bows of the coaster in mountainous seas. We gradually got closer and closer. I could see the anxious faces of the crew on the coaster's fo'c'sle, or forecastle. They were eyeing the rapidly closing gap between the two ships with obvious trepidation.

Suddenly, a big swell lifted the coaster's bows out of the water. Looking at the massive green wall of water, it was obvious what was going to happen. The officer shouted, “Clear the quarterdeck!” He was shouting to himself, as the rest of us were already heading for'ard out of the way. As the lieutenant ran to join us, the coaster’s bows crashed down onto our deck and sliced through the starboard quarter. The screech of grinding steel interrupted the noise of the wind, and the bows slid out, leaving a big, gaping hole fringed with twisted metal.

The ship went ahead and we drew away. Everyone breathed a collective sigh of relief. Then, like the cavalry to the rescue, the Dover lifeboat arrived. I turned to my oppo, or friend, and said, "You have to admire those men."

"Yeah," he said. "Our two-and-a-half-thousand-ton frigate is bein' chucked all over the place, an' they come out in a little boat." Then someone threw them a line, which they took across to the coaster, and eventually we managed to get the towing hawser across.

Morning came, the sea eased, and we arrived at Dover Harbour, where a tug brought the coaster alongside the harbour wall. The seaboat was sent over, so that their captain could sign the salvage papers. I was bowman of the boat, so I was able to go on board the coaster and see it for myself. The press had arrived, and the coxswain and I were happy to oblige for a photograph with the captain's young son, who had been on board. The captain had been taking his wife and son on passage with him, and they looked relieved and happy as we sat on their fo'c'sle. The photograph was published in the *Daily Telegraph*, though I've lost it now.

I never did receive my share of the salvage money. However, I did enjoy the extra time ashore that followed from having to go into dry dock to have the damage repaired. We sailed into the dry dock, which was still full of water. Then the gates were closed and the water pumped out. Dockyard mateys (workers) positioned timbers between the ship's side and the dockyard wall, holding the ship upright as the keel settled on the dock bottom. Then a little army of welders and fitters and so on descended on the ship to start cutting out the damaged steel plates. This wasn't the only time that we had to be patched up by the dockyard, though.

We were tied up alongside the jetty in Portsmouth dockyard. I was the bosun's mate manning the gangway with the quartermaster, during the morning watch. A Tribal class frigate was due to come alongside us, and we'd called a couple of the duty watch to take their lines to tie up. This was routine stuff, and we watched with casual interest as she approached.

"Funny sort of approach," I said.

"Mmm, is a bit," answered the QM, taking a sip from his mug of tea.

Normally, a ship coming alongside another ship approaches at an oblique angle, which varies according to such factors as the wind and tide and how much room there is to manoeuvre. But she was approaching bows on at a right angle, and I puzzled over how her captain was going to turn the ship through ninety degrees on the spot. *Bloody impossible*, I thought. She approached closer and closer, to within a few feet.

"Shall I get a fender?" I joked.

"Need more than a sodding fender," replied the QM, as the Tribal went astern and slid away from us. Then, instead of going around and making a proper approach, she came back at exactly the same angle, but this time faster. We watched in goggle-eyed amazement as it became obvious that she was going to ram into our side. I hit the action stations alarm, and the QM shouted, "Hands to emergency stations" over the tannoy.

The frigate's bows sliced into our side and crashed through the radio operator's mess, where men had been sleeping a few seconds earlier. By now, people had appeared from everywhere and were watching, as the Tribal class frigate disengaged and finally came back and alongside. When I looked at the damage later, I was shocked to see how close an escape some of the radio operators had had. The bunks, which lined the ship's side, were twisted wrecks, and anyone in them would have died. Curiously, the damage was neatly separated between the original deck and the one added on years later. The radio operator's mess was situated on what had originally been HMS Grenville's upper deck when she was built as a destroyer in World War II. This additional deck had been smashed right through by the Tribal's bow, but the original ship's side and deck below this was relatively undamaged. You could have driven a car through the hole, so we were destined for dry dock again.

Later in the day, the captain of the Tribal class frigate (whose name I confess to have forgotten) sent every mess a crate of beer. This was welcome, though if I'd been one of the radio operator's mess, I doubt my forgiveness could have been bought that easily. I've often wondered what happened to their captain. Presumably, he would have faced a court martial - though he's probably a bloody admiral now.

Going to sea was out of the question, so I was able to get away on weekend leave. I used to enjoy going for a drink at the Bell Inn in Kingsteignton. The landlord, Fred, was an ex-Navy gunnery instructor. Needless to say, news of the collision had preceded me via the six o'clock news, and I was held personally accountable. As I walked into the bar, Fred, the landlord of the pub, called out, "Hello, Crunch! Hear you've smashed up your ship." He fell about laughing. Then Jake, one of the pub regulars, joined in with some more friendly banter at my expense.

I enjoyed chatting to Jake. He'd been in a cavalry (armoured) regiment during World War II and the Korean War. He was a bit of a character, and he used to tell excellent stories. Whether these stories gained a bit in the telling is a moot point; but who cares?

He told me that the soap received in parcels sent from the UK during the Korean War used to float. When the troops went down to the river to wash, he sometimes lost his soap, which would float away. So he wrote a tongue-in-cheek letter of complaint to the soap's manufacturers. In return, he received a little parcel offering the firm's best wishes and a tiny anchor and chain to attach to his bar of soap.

Jake recounted one tale with particular relish. His eyes lit up, and the pub's parrot, which was sat on his shoulder, shit down the back of his jumper. Jake pretended not to notice and scratched the parrot's neck.

"A few years ago, I was up in front of the magistrate on a minor charge. The beak didn't like the tone of some of my answers, and he looks towards me and says, 'Mr. ----, are you trying to show your contempt for this court?' So I replied, 'On the contrary your honour, I'm trying very hard to conceal it.' Then the bastard jailed me."

Trying not to be outdone, I told him the Navy's standing joke about the Splash Target Coxswain. A splash target is a wooden frame with metal scoops, which, when towed through the sea, throws a fountain of water in the air. The target is towed a long way behind a ship to provide a cheap but effective moving target for other ships to fire at.

The target is laid out on the quarterdeck, a chair is lashed on to the top of it, and a volunteer is sought to be the coxswain. If someone sufficiently new and gullible enough can be found, he is briefed on how to signal back the fall of shot and given a set of semaphore flags. Then he is told to dress appropriately. The attire would be something like a diver's wetsuit, plus breathing apparatus, and anything else that came to mind. The final stage was to lash the coxswain onto the chair and lower him over the side.

By this time, usually even the most credulous would see through the joke. Though a senior AB told me that a couple of years earlier, one young lad practically had to be restrained from staying on the seat and still didn't get it until the target was brought back on board with just a few tiny scraps of seat fabric still attached.

Normally, the splash target was stowed out of the way against a bulkhead, whilst the towing wire was kept on a revolving drum on the quarterdeck. Streaming the target and then winching it back was a straightforward task, and generally the quarterdeck PO took charge. Not so on one occasion, though. Halfway through proceedings, a sub-lieutenant came and insisted on operating the brake that controlled the wire as it unreeled off the drum. The target streamed further and further astern, throwing a big spout of water up into the air. The end of the wire was not attached to the drum, so you needed to apply the brake before the end was reached. He obviously didn't know this, and the end of the wire disappeared astern and followed the splash target to the bottom of the sea. Jake fell about laughing, and then we carried on chatting, discussing service life, and had a few more beers.

The amount of alcohol I drank gradually increased. This was not unusual in an environment where heavy drinking was the norm. So long as you did your work and avoided causing trouble, no one would interfere. I sometimes went to the cinema or had a cup of tea and something to eat in Aggie Westons or the Fleet Club, which had originally been established by the Victorians to provide alternatives to the demon drink. But normally, I spent every penny I had over the bar of various public houses in time-honoured Royal Navy tradition.

One evening, however, I managed to get myself into some bother. A friend was celebrating his eighteenth birthday, and after a skinful of beer, a few of us wandered back through the dockyard towards the ship. In their drunken stupidity, the others decided to use some forty-gallon oil drums as depth charges to sink the U boats (wooden catamarans) tied to the dock wall.

"Fire depth charges," one of the lads shouted.

"Bombs away!" someone else howled, as the oil drums bounced off the catamaran. I should have cleared off, but I stupidly just stood there.

Then - surprise, surprise - the dockyard police arrived and everyone ran for it, including me. I went about four paces, then tripped over a steam pipe, and got nabbed by the dockyard police. The bobby lifted me up from the floor.

"You alright, mate?" he asked. He could see that I wasn't going to be any problem and sat me in a patrol car, along with the only other idiot to have got caught. The end result of this, apart from some minor cuts and bruises to my face, was that I was put on defaulters. A few days later, I was in front of the captain, where I protested my innocence. The charge was causing a hazard to navigation and being drunk and disorderly in Her Majesty's dockyard. I was fined. I can't remember how much, but it was a painfully large fine, which had me joining the ranks of the teetotallers for an extended period. With hindsight, it's a shame that this and similar incidents didn't make me wake up to the fact that I was unconsciously following in my father's footsteps and developing an alcohol problem.

In the early part of 1973, I volunteered for the job of working with the Artificers' department. I took over the routine maintenance of the twin 40mm Bofors gun. It was a chance to be my own boss, and I thoroughly enjoyed myself. I had the series of maintenance schedules and books for the gun—a bit like a servicing manual on a car. Every morning I took the manuals and did routine jobs such as cleaning the barrels or stripping and cleaning the breech. If I needed help or advice I could ask the chief artificer in charge, though generally he left me to get on with things in my own time. It was good to have a break from the routine of scrubbing and painting. One of my new duties was to inspect the magazine and the armoury every day, record the temperature, and check that everything was stowed away correctly. Unfortunately, one day I closed the armoury door and left, leaving it unlocked in my haste to finish. The officer of the day discovered it and sent for me, though to my amazement I was just given a telling off and not formally put on defaulters.

Shipboard life went on with its alternating boredom and excitement. We enjoyed the odd foreign visit to European ports and looked on enviously as other ships left for more exotic destinations like the Far East or West Indies. Once, whilst at sea, a rating reported to the sick bay with diarrhoea and vomiting. He was diagnosed with food poisoning and put to bed in the sick bay under the care of the leading medical attendant. A few more cases also received similar tender loving care. I started feeling bad, too, and made a sudden dash for the heads, colliding with another guy on the same mission. Five minutes later, one of the lads saw me in the Burma Way (central corridor) and looked at my pale features. "Not too well, Scouse?" he asked.

"No, mate," I replied. "I could shit through the eye of a needle!"

I went to the sick bay, butwhen it became obvious that the majority of the crew was affected, it was work as normal. So lots of dismal, pasty-faced sailors shuffled around doing tasks that took far longer than usual, whilst the heads were worked overtime.

A more welcome diversion was provided by a visit to HMS Excellent, the gunnery school at Whale Island. Some of the crew were designated as landing parties, which could be sent ashore in times of civil unrest to provide backup for the civil authorities. This was something of a relic of Empire. The training felt like something from a different age, though I took it seriously enough. The main drill consisted of the landing party forming a hollow square, like Wellington's soldiers at Waterloo, though they had faced Napoleons cavalry instead of rioters.

The officer in charge stood in the middle with the men carrying the banner; the remainder of us formed the square, facing outwards. We wore No8 denim working rig and boots, and carried rifles with fixed bayonets. Instead of our normal caps, we put on outdated steel helmets, which in my case wobbled precariously every time I marched forwards. Then the two banner men would unroll their banner, proclaiming something to the effect that, "This is an illegal assembly, disperse at once." If the rioters failed to disperse as ordered, they displayed the reverse of the banner, which warned that we were about to open fire. If all this failed, the rank facing the rioters kneeled, and one man would be ordered to shoot one of the ringleaders. This was my job, and I looked forward to the ship being deployed to some trouble spot and getting my chance to bag a rioter, though unfortunately it never happened.

Chapter Seven

In August 1973, I was drafted to HMS Cambridge, the gunnery range near Plymouth. Having been there before on a gunnery course, I anticipated enjoying my time amongst the peace and quiet of the south Devon countryside. This time I was to be ship's company, part of the permanent staff who run the firing range.

Most days, the guns were engaged in anti-aircraft practice. The 4.5-inch guns banged away at red fabric sleeve targets, towed behind ageing Hawker Hunter jet fighters, coming in low from the sea towards the guns on the cliff. The shells would explode with a satisfying bang and a cloud of dense, black smoke. The locals in the bungalows next to the camp delighted in pointing out that the shells always missed. But the shells had proximity fuses, which exploded before hitting the target, spraying out a lethal hail of shrapnel, increasing the chances of bringing down aircraft. On rare occasions, a shell would sever the towing cable. Then we'd wait for low tide and clamber over the rocky foreshore to retrieve the target.

Sometimes I would go out with another rating on one of the RAF's Air Sea Rescue launches, based at RAF Mountbatten. Our task was to spot the fall of shot for the guns when they were firing at a surface target. We would radio back whether the shot landed over or short. Not exactly arduous work, given the frequent mists or wandering small yachts that interrupted the day's shoot. This left us free to concentrate on the more pressing issue of catching mackerel with the fishing rods we took along.

The RAF crews were a good bunch, always ready with a joke or a hot brew. We joined some of the crew for a lunchtime drink one day in a pub near their camp. Most of them went back on time, but one lad, determined to maintain the RAF's honour, decided to stay on and keep drinking with us. We carried him back to his camp later in the afternoon. A passing RAF warrant officer threw him in the back of his car, after throwing a few choice words in our direction. Discretion being the better part of valour, we abandoned our new chum to the RAF's discipline and beat a hasty retreat back to HMS Cambridge.

We spent hours on cleaning and maintenance duties for the chief bosun's mate, a corpulent West Countryman with a scraggly beard. One way of avoiding work was to get him chatting, which wasn't difficult. He told us one story, swearing it was true, though I confess to having doubts.

"One day I gets a call from a lady living in one of the bungalows next to camp," he said. "She reckoned that she could see naked men in the barrack blocks and wasn't happy about it."

He carried on in his broad West Country accent. "Now, being keen to keep the natives happy, I goes round there to investigate—then she invited me into the living room for a look, and I told her politely that I couldn't see how it was possible."

Then he continued, mimicking an irate civvy lady's voice, "She said, 'Yes, you can, put a stool on top of the table, stand on it, and you can see right inside the rooms!'"

Everyone laughed dutifully, and the conversation moved on to something less amusing, homosexuality, which was illegal in the

Royal Navy at that time. I chatted to the lads about something that was troubling me a little. I'd been temporarily put in a mess with some wardroom (officer's) stewards.

"Lads, judging by the stewards' conversation, I reckon their relationship with one officer is based on *queen's* regulations," I said, emphasising the word *queen's*. This was an allusion to Queen's Regulations and Admiralty Instructions, which govern conduct, and it got a laugh. I suppose I ought to have reported my suspicions formally. But I kept my thoughts to myself, though I was relieved when I was moved to another mess with the rest of the ship's company gunnery ratings.

The other incident was more serious. It happened on board HMS Grenville. One of the petty officers (the stores accountant, if I remember correctly) was suddenly sent ashore without warning. Rumours abounded, but it seemed that he'd gone into the junior seaman's mess and molested one of the juniors in his hammock. The result was loss of rank, loss of pension, and a dishonourable discharge from the Navy.

-

In September 1973, I was drafted to Whale Island on a gunnery course. The name conjured up visions of some remote and barren Arctic outpost. The reality was a little closer to home. HMS Excellent, the Royal Navy Gunnery School, was on Whale Island. But it was only an island at high tide, when the estuary waters covered up the muddy creek that separated the island from mainland Portsmouth.

I dragged my suitcase and kitbag over the bridge and reported to the guardroom. Of course, being Sunday, no one was in the least bit interested in me. Routine took over, though, and I was allocated to a messdeck and given bedding. By now, being a master in the art of wasting time, I was capable of dragging a joining routine out over two days. It was easy to ensure I arrived at somewhere like the pay office just before it closed, or skipped discreetly backwards in a queue until tea break, and so on. But as Sunday was my free time, I raced around and got it finished quickly.

The next morning, I paraded with the rest of the lads. We were reminded of the name of the course, as if we didn't know; we were to be trained as specialists (second class) in gunnery fire control. At this time, the gunnery branch was still nominally divided into two main divisions. The Quarters ratings manned and loaded the guns, and Fire Control ratings manned the various radars, predictors, and directors used to aim the guns and missiles. But both sides worked together in symbiosis to achieve the rapid and accurate gunnery for which the Royal Navy was long famous.

Gunnery ratings carry out the Navy's ceremonial duties, so we had interminable parade training. It was no different than the drill we learned in basic training. There was just a lot more of it, conducted by gunnery instructors with voices that carried like thunder across the big asphalt parade ground. Just across the road in a protective shelter was the gun carriage used to carry Queen Victoria's coffin at her funeral—pulled by gunnery ratings. We were proud to be part of such tradition, but happy in practice to keep personal involvement to a minimum. One course each year had to do the annual service of remembrance at the Cenotaph in London, known to those who spent endless weeks drilling on the parade ground as the November Handicaps. We were all delighted to learn that we would be spared this; the privilege went to another course.

The course progressed between the parade ground, the classroom (where we learnt gunnery theory), and Fraser Gunnery Range. Having served on a ship that was a relic of the Second World War, most modern equipment was new to me.

Radar sets determined the range and direction of a target, and translated this into a bearing and elevation for the guns. My favourite place was the gun director, located high up on a ship's superstructure, where the guns could be aimed using the old-fashioned, but personally satisfying, optical sights. The director was a bin-shaped structure which could rotate to aim the gunsight on any bearing. Guns were all aimed from here before the introduction of radar controlled gunnery, but the optical sight was kept as a backup system in the event that technology failed us.

We drilled interminably on 4.5-inch guns, the main armament of the frigates and destroyers which made up the bulk of the Navy's surface fleet. We also trained on the 40mm Bofors gun and the 20mm Oerlikon, which were really World War II-era weapons, and useless against fast jets.

Someone asked one of the gunnery instructors why we trained on older weapons. The answer was straightforward: It's simply wasteful to fire an expensive missile across the bows or into, say, a small vessel smuggling drugs or a pirate. The Bofors did the job cheaply and efficiently.

Eventually we went to HMS Cambridge for the final phase of live firing. I spent many long hours sat in the gun director, watching a surface target appear and disappear in the mist and haze of a warm Devon summer. One day I was sat in the director enjoying a period of inactivity. Not the gunnery officer, though. The target was clearly identified on radar and capable of being engaged, but peacetime range safety rules didn't allow it, unless the director aimer could actually see it through his optical sight.

Then the mist cleared a little and the target came into view. I could hear in my headset that the gunnery officer had seen it through his sight on the bridge. The transmitting station crew still had it acquired on radar and predictor. The order, “Salvos!” came through, and the gun crews loaded and rammed surface practice shells in the twin barrels of the 4.5-inch turret. The gun turret swung around, following the radar on the side of my director, and the order, “engage,” echoed through the system.

Whilst all this was going on, the mist started to close in, as sea mists are wont to do, and the image of the target in my sight became a little indistinct. A sense of mischief took over, and I hit the switch that broke the firing circuit and shouted, “Lost target!” down the mike. This wasn’t strictly true, but the rage and frustration in the gunnery officer’s voice was a treat to hear.

“What the fuck do you mean, lost target?” he howled through my headset.

"Lost in the mist, sir," I replied.

The gunnery officer's voice took on a slow, threatening tone. "I-can-see-it-as-clear-as-day."

I knew I was sailing close to the wind, but couldn't resist winding him up. "Sorry, sir can't see it anymore," I said, smiling happily. He knew that the magnification of his sight was higher than mine, so he had to allow me the benefit of the doubt.

I incurred the great man's wrath again a few weeks later. Security had been tightened due to the troubles in Northern Ireland. Anyone bringing a car into the main camp had to have previously registered it in a nice new book kept in the quartermaster's lobby.

This was a response to incidents in Belfast, where the provisional IRA had taken families hostage and then blackmailed someone in the security forces into driving one of their cars, which had been packed full of explosives. I was on guard duty the morning the new scheme was put into operation. Clutching the book, I waved all the registered cars through the gate without problem. My orders that morning from the duty petty officer were clear: "If it ain't in the book, it don't come in - no exceptions."

An Able Seaman arrived on his battered old scooter, which was unregistered. He pleaded, and I went into the quartermaster's lobby to try to sort things out for him.

"You've had your instructions," was the duty PO's reply. So the Able Seaman had to park out of camp and walk back. Then the gunnery officer arrived in a car. I checked the book and saw that it wasn't registered. He gave me some load of old bollocks about having to use his wife's car that morning, and I listened respectfully and attentively. Then, ignoring the frantic 'Let him through!' gestures coming from the duty PO, I closed the barrier, sending him back out of camp.

The words *Thank you, God* went through my mind, and I saluted the gunnery officer's departure to the sound of clashing gears and muttered curses. Later in the day, the fleet chief petty officer, who was in charge of the ranges, summoned me. No amount of flak would have spoilt my little bit of egalitarian fun, but I was congratulated for having done my job properly and fairly.

I had plenty of fun socially, too. One of my mates, the very Caucasian Leading Seaman Nye, had the very politically incorrect nickname of Nigger Nye. His show-stopping party trick, which he demonstrated one evening in the bar, was to eat glass. He took a pint glass, bit a chunk off, chewed it, and then swallowed the pieces. The whole glass, with the exception of the thick base, went the same way. Then he went on to tell us more about his glass-eating exploits.

Nigger told us he was "on a run ashore one evening when I met some Yankee matelots to whom I kindly demonstrated the art. One of them insisted on having a go, too, and ended up on the deck spewing blood." He confessed this with a wicked grin and admitted to not telling them that the trick was to chew the glass until it went into little pieces, at which point it was safe to eat.

Soon I was back to Portsmouth, having completed my 2s, or Fire Controller 2nd Class, course. The next step was a Seacat missile aimer's course, which consisted of two weeks spent indoors practising on a simulator. The only tangible benefit was a nice shiny rocket badge on my best No1 uniform; unfortunately, it wasn't a course that earned extra pay.

Chapter Eight

I was sent back to HMS Cambridge to await a draft to sea. One morning, the summons arrived to report to the regulating office.

The RPO said, "You've got a draft chit—HMS Danae, you lucky git."

"Why is that so lucky?" I asked.

"Because she's in Australia, and you'll be flying out to Sydney to join her," he said.

This was too good to be true. A few days later, I was told my RAF flight to Australia had been cancelled. The Greeks and Turks were fighting each other in Cyprus, and extra transport aircraft had been diverted to duties at Akrotiri, the RAF airfield on the island. A few weeks later, another summons to the regulating office brought me the splendid news that I would be joining HMS Danae in

Thailand. I hardly knew where Thailand was, but it was vaguely eastern and surely exotic.

Then the bloody Greeks and Turks decided to have another go at each other and my flight was cancelled yet again. In return, I vowed a lifetime boycott of halva, kebabs, and anything else remotely connected to either side. Eventually, I did join my ship after flying from RAF Brize Norton to Singapore, via a short stopover in the Maldives Islands. On arrival, I discovered that HMS Danae was at sea, so I was sent to Terror Barracks, part of the British naval base.

I was put in an empty room with a broken punkah (fan), on the upper floor of an old colonial-style barrack block, but otherwise left to take care of myself. This was fine by me, and I spent my time in the NAAFI bar keeping well clear of any working parties.

The heat and humidity were a shock to the system. The broken punkah on the ceiling of my room didn't help, but eventually I started to acclimatise and enjoy the new environment. My own method of doing this was to sit in the bar doing nothing but drinking bottles of very cold Tiger beer until my money ran out.

I was fascinated by the chit chats (lizards) that ran up the walls or clung to the ceilings. The Bombay Runners were less appealing. These huge tropical cockroaches made my old chums on HMS Grenville look tiny by comparison. On occasion, drunken matelots would have competitions to see who could be the first one to catch a live chit chat and bite its head off. I never witnessed this myself - and I'm glad, too.

One afternoon, I decided to take a trip into Singapore City. I hailed a tri-shaw, a three-wheeled bicycle with a passenger seat, and asked to be taken to Raffles, the famous hotel named after Sir Thomas Raffles, the British colonial administrator who founded Singapore in 1819. Being a bit green in the ways of the East, it never occurred to me to bargain for the fare before setting off. When we arrived, the driver asked for a huge sum of money, which I didn't have. I stupidly gave him most of my cash, not realising that I'd paid way over the going price. So there you are, not such a salty old sea dog as I'd fancied myself.

After a couple of weeks, my nice little skive in Terror Barracks came to an end. HMS Danae arrived in the dockyard, and I was given a berth in the for'ard seamen's mess: New ship, new messmates, new routines; a lot to learn and get accustomed to. Danae was a Leander class frigate, launched in October 1965. She wasn't the latest warship afloat, but with a twin 4.5-inch gun turret for'ard, a Seacat missile launcher aft and a Wasp helicopter for anti-submarine warfare, she was a proper fighting warship.

Like HMS Grenville, Danae carried a Chinese laundry team. These Cantonese civilians worked, ate, cooked, and slept in the tiny laundry down aft, near the quarterdeck. Most of the dhobey wallahs spoke very little English and kept to themselves. They had names, of course, but in time-honoured Navy tradition, we referred to them by numbers. The boss was called Number 1, the second in command Number 2, and so on. There was also a Chinese tailor, who lived in a tiny locker near the funnel with his colleague, the cobbler. These two industrious guys produced made-to-measure shoes and suits. They stayed with us until we returned to England, where they transferred to another ship going back out to the Far East.

Aside from the purchase of a duty-free Seiko watch from the NAAFI, which would last for twenty years, my other souvenir of the visit was another tattoo. I went with Yorkie Cutts, a greenie (electrician), to Johnny Ghurkha's Tattoo Emporium in Nee Soon. Yorkie had a pair of eyes tattooed on his arse. It seemed a bit extreme to me, so I settled for something nautically conventional, a sailing ship on my left forearm.

All too soon, it was time to leave Singapore. Dressed in best tropical whites, we left harbour in brilliant sunshine, our destination the Seychelles in the Indian Ocean. The voyage quickly settled into the usual routine of watchkeeping and working part of ship, interspersed with action station exercises. Duties such as lifebuoy ghost and bridge lookout were a joy, with sea and sky of intense vivid colours, and flying fish for entertainment.

We anchored off one of the many Maldives Islands en route and got a tantalising glimpse of palm-fringed beaches and dazzling silver sand. Sadly, we weren't allowed to go ashore. Two hundred matelots wandering around a tiny tropical island was considered too much of a risk - to flora, fauna, and the local female population.

The Seychelles didn't prove disappointing, though. We tied up alongside the jetty near the capital of Victoria. The town seemed pleasant, with some nice old colonial-looking buildings and a statue of Queen Victoria.

One evening, I found myself detailed off as a member of a three-man shore patrol, assuming the temporary role of ship's policeman, keeping an eye on the activities of my oppos ashore. We reported to the police station to collect a local policeman to work with us. I don't know why we had to put a patrol ashore; it wasn't usual. But it seemed a big improvement to duty watch on board, spending four tedious hours stood by the gangway as bosun's mate.

Always willing to combine pleasure with business, we settled ourselves in various bars, the better to keep an eye on our off-watch brethren. The local bobby was clearly uncomfortable sitting around drinking whilst on duty. We had no such scruples and knocked back a respectable but manageable quantity of beer. The thought then arose that we might best do our duty by going to a dodgy nightclub, where many of the lads had gathered by now. The local plod drew the line at this and left us to our own devices.

We entered the club, convincing the doorman with our Naval Patrol armbands to admit us *gratis* in order to 'maintain law and order'. Inside, it was lively but as respectable and law-abiding as a clergymen's convention. The one notable exception was Peter C., the master-at-arms. He held a position analogous to the regimental sergeant major in an Army regiment, and was respected as a firm but decent guy.

Peter was as drunk as a skunk, or to use a really old naval term, half seas over. Being good-natured in his drink, he let me half walk and half carry him back on board. He staggered up the gangway and eventually fell into his bunk, with the mother of all hangovers to come. Peter came from Newton Abbot, which was my new domicile, and we were later to become good mates.

Visiting the Seychelles was a marvellous opportunity to walk on unspoilt tropical beaches, see unusual wildlife, and dive in crystal clear waters. Instead, like most of my mates, I wasted my time, consuming the maximum amount of alcohol at the lowest possible price. There were a couple of notable exceptions. Two ABs, one of whom came from the Republic of Ireland, were teetotallers. These strange creatures used to go ashore together and engage in cultural pursuits, to the mystification of the rest of us.

It might seem surprising that there was a foreign national serving onboard one of HM ships, but it's quite common. On the HMS Grenville, all the wardroom stewards were locally-enlisted personnel from Malta. They were a good bunch who taught me interesting phrases in Maltese, such as "I'm going to fuck your mother" - guaranteed to liven up the proceedings in any Maltese bar.

Before leaving the Seychelles, the stoker's, or marine engineer's, mess decided to organise a banyan. Dressed in silly costumes, loaded with beer and something to barbecue, they sailed away in the ship's whaler towards some remote and tranquil beach. Sadly for them, but much to the later amusement of the rest of the ship's company, they managed to shipwreck the whaler on a reef and had to swim ashore.

Though I might be giving the impression that we were engaged in a paid version of a Cunard cruise, in reality we worked hard, especially the bulk of the ship's company, such as the seamen and stokers, who did four-hour duty watches through the night in addition to working during the day. There were gunnery drills, firefighting exercises, seamanship manoeuvres, and so on. Only one night out of four was a full night's sleep, and that was never guaranteed.

Our next port of call was South Africa. HMS Danae sailed in to the former British naval base at Simonstown. Swarms of black dockyard workers came on board to help with the many minor repairs and maintenance jobs. This was the time that I'd starting developing a social conscience - an awkward thing at times. I went through the processof questioning authority and prevalent ideas that most young people go through. And I joined Friends of the Earth and wrote a few letters to various governments for Amnesty International's campaigns on behalf of political prisoners. It gave me a feeling of satisfaction to be involved, even in a small way, in helping humanitarian causes. But it never interfered with my real job, as a work-hard-play-hard servant of Queen and country, as I saw it then.

Most impacting, though, was when I went ashore and saw apartheid in action. It certainly wasn't something I approved of. The ugliest aspects weren't visible on a short visit, but we saw the lesser features, such as separate railway carriages and benches. We delighted in flouting this, sitting on blacks-only seats, sharing conversation with black people, who probably saw us as a nuisance and likely to get them into trouble. Still, I found the black people friendly, and I enjoyed chatting with some of the black dockyard workers who came onboard HMS Danae in the dockyard.

No visit to South Africa would be complete without a trip to Cape Town's Table Mountain - at least according to the tourist office. Like most of my mates, I gave it a miss and went for a late night trip to the shebeens of the notorious and dangerous District 6. A shebeen is (or was) an illegal drinking den, and definitely the sort of place in which to get in a fight or get robbed. I managed to avoid both, but one evening of District 6 was enough for my taste. It was rough by any standard, and whilst I liked to put on the tough, hard-drinking serviceman image, the safer, more comfortable white bars in the city were really more to my taste.

But for me, the best part of the visit was range practice. Being a gunner, I was meant to maintain a certain degree of proficiency with small arms. One morning, the gunnery officer arranged for the gunners to march out to the firing ranges near Simonstown. It wasn't a wilderness, but it seemed a huge expanse of African bush, and I relished marching along the deserted tracks between high kopjes under a clear blue sky.

In competition with the rest of the lads, I distinguished myself as the best shot, which I was as modest about then as I am now. A barbecue with huge steaks followed this exercise. What a wonderful day, maybe one of the best ones I ever had in the Navy. I can still feel the recoil of the rifle smacking into my shoulder and almost taste the cordite as the spent cartridges ejected. I've been back to Africa many times since, but the sky is never quite so clear nor the smell of the grass so sweet as then.

The voyage back to England was memorable, too. Traditionally, ships returning from the Far East have a sod's opera. Each mess puts on an act or comic sketch in a concert. The for'ard seamen's mess decided to do a short, and very alternative, version of

Cinderella, and I was asked to take part. This didn't appeal, but the lure of being excused watchkeeping did.

On the night of the performance, it was a different story, and I regretted agreeing to it. In an effort to placate my nerves, I had a little drop of Cape Smoke, the strong South African brandy that I'd smuggled onboard in Africa. One 'small drink' followed another, and my artistic fears disappeared; half an hour and half a bottle later, I was near legless.

On the quarterdeck, the ship's company was enjoying the show, with the captain and officers sat in the front row. When my mess staged its sketch, I forgot the script and wandered around in a hazy nightmare under the suspicious gaze of the captain, who I later learned couldn't quite decide if I was drunk or part of some surreal comedic plot. Then, for my *pièce de résistance*, I fell backwards through the guardrails and would have fallen into the sea but for the quick reactions of a couple of lads who caught me, to the ironic applause of the audience.

A few days before we arrived back home, something happened that reminded me of the gulf between myself and some of those in positions of command. Every day, a typewritten sheet of daily orders was published, detailing the daily routine and duties, plus news and announcements. This one included a word from the captain, something along the lines of "We'll be returning to our home port soon, so you should all have haircuts, as your families won't welcome you with long or scruffy hair." I knew my family would welcome me if I returned in a grass skirt with hair down to my waist. *What nonsense runs through the senior commissioned mind* was the thought that went through mine. But officers came from a very different social and economic background than me, and we viewed the world through equally different eyes.

The majority of our officers had been to Dartmouth, as midshipmen, before being commissioned. They socialised in the Wardroom, which an officer once told me was considered to be the most exclusive gentlemen's club in the world: Arguably so, but there was no doubt that their living conditions were immensely superior to our cramped life on a typical messdeck.

There was a story, apocryphal perhaps, that someone measured a messdeck and then wrote in to *Pig Farmers Weekly,* asking how many pigs could be kept in an area of that size. Supposedly, the number given was far less than the number of sailors living in the mess.

Of course, I was never naïve enough to imagine everyone living like maritime Marxists, sharing everything equally. "RHIP," or rank, "has its privileges" was a much quoted maxim, and, up to a point, I tended to agree.

Once, we were given questionnaires to fill out, much of which I've forgotten. One question sticks in my mind: We were asked if, with an eye to future warship design, we would accept reduced living space in order to accommodate more weapon systems. It seemed hard to imagine how we could live in a much smaller space, so I suggested -anonymously, of course - that the officers lose their baths and the captain lose his spacious cabins.

Chapter Nine

The usual round of leave and courses followed the return to England, whilst the ship underwent repairs and maintenance in the dockyard. At various times I went on firefighting, disaster control, and safety equipment courses. They were usually interesting and often good fun.

A helicopter handling and firefighting course included flight deck duties with a Wasp helicopter, carried by Leander class frigates for anti-submarine work. Lashing down the chopper as it came into land on a pitching and rolling flight deck was normally the task of the Fleet Air Arm ratings. But some of the seamen were also taught how to run in under the rotors as the chopper landed, attaching a strop from a strongpoint on deck to an anchor point above each of the chopper's four wheels. The strop was then pulled tight, holding the chopper safely down, regardless of the angle of the flight deck. It sounds easy, but it can get a bit tricky in rough weather.

Another enjoyable course was firefighting at HMS Phoenix, near Portsmouth. We learned how to use breathing apparatuses to go into smoke-filled compartments to extinguish fires and rescue the injured. There were exercises with real fires, lit under controlled conditions, which we would put out using hoses or handheld fire extinguishers. The fires were started with either solid fuel or oil, which was poured into deep metal trays. The oil burnt with thick, black acrid smoke, which blackened everything it came into contact with - including me. Going into a smoke-filled chamber with flames leaping up into the air was a thought-provoking experience. Standing there gripping a bucking hose and watching the spray through the limited view of the face mask of the breathing apparatus, it wasn't hard to imagine doing it for real inside a blazing, shell-torn warship in battle.

One rather sobering moment occurred in the classroom. The Navy was due to replace our heavier cotton/denim No8 working uniforms with a new easy-to-wash, easy-to-iron lightweight manmade fibre. One of the petty officer instructors took a sample of the new material and put a match to it. It flared up immediately, dropping blobs of melted fabric on the classroom floor. "What do you think of that?" he challenged.

We all made the obvious comments on the dangers of wearing anything made of it near a fire. Sadly, a few years later, our words were to be borne out during the Falklands War. Some Royal Navy ships were hit by Exocet missiles, including HMS Sheffield, which was sunk. The missiles were launched from Argentinean Super Étendard aeroplanes. Not surprisingly, when they exploded they started fires. Then a number of men were injured when their clothes caught fire, with the new fabric melting into their wounds and exacerbating their injuries.

One change of uniform that did seem sensible was the issue of berets. Previously, we'd worn the traditional white naval cap, even with working dress, but a beret was much handier and easier to keep clean.

By now I was nearly twenty, and pushing for promotion. So I was temporarily drafted to a Tribal class frigate, to take the category 441 tests in seamanship for promotion to leading seaman. I joined HMS Mohawk in Rosyth, whilst the Cod War was being 'fought' between Britain and Iceland. It was a dispute over access to Arctic fishing areas. Beyond that, I knew little and cared even less, being happy to go and do whatever was required of me.

HMS Mohawk sailed north to the Arctic on fishery protection duties, and I received extra tuition in seamanship and then took and passed the various 441s. We saw nothing of the Icelandic gunboats, but we did have some runs ashore in Norway, which was notable for beautiful scenery and ruinously expensive beer.

We were also in the area where the trawler Gaul vanished in a force-ten gale, seventy miles north of Norway. Rumour had it that the Gaul's nets were snagged by a submarine or that it was sunk by the Russians who mistook her for a spy trawler; many of their own trawlers were involved in monitoring signals intelligence and covert activities.

A couple of weeks later I rejoined HMS Danae, and was then sent to HMS Raleigh for the leading seaman's promotion course and examination, which I modestly admit to passing with flying colours. Then, just before my twentieth birthday, I received my promotion. I sailed over the heads of my older and longer-serving peers. The start of a brilliant career, you might think. Not so; in a pattern that would tend to repeat itself, I immediately cocked things up.

HMS Danae had a ship's dance at the Talk of the Town in Union Street, Plymouth. As the ship's newest and most junior killick, I was stiffed for the job of taking charge of the shore patrol.

On the night of the dance, we dressed in No1 uniform with boots, white anklets and belts, plus naval patrol armbands. Then we sat in a small side room, whilst the ship's company, accompanied by wives and girlfriends (but not both), danced and partied. All would have been well if not for the generosity of the waitress making the punch. The two ABs who were supposedly under my command had a couple of drinks in moderation. But I just didn't know when to stop.

My next memory is of standing on the brow (gangway) of the ship, saluting and swaying back and forth, before somehow finding my way to my bunk, oblivious to the fact that I'd been sent back early in a taxi.

Retribution came quickly, and a few days later, I found myself on captain's defaulters. The familiar sound of, "Quick march - left, right, left, right, left . . . right turn, off caps," brought me in front of the captain's table.

"Widders," he said, looking at me wearily, "your promotion is hanging in the balance. You need to sort yourself out."

I couldn't help agreeing with him, though I kept my comments to a simple, "Yes, sir." A formal admonishment followed, which went on my record. The master-at-arms then shouted, "On caps, left turn, quick march!" and I went off to do some serious thinking.

One of the petty officers had already told me that he was fed up with my tendency to answer back and have the last word. That was on top of a similar talk from Lieutenant L., my divisional officer. They had my interests at heart and knew I'd settle down once I did some more growing up and thought less about the perks of promotion and more about the responsibilities. Deep down I knew they were right, and I appreciated their concern for me. So I wound my neck in, shut my mouth, and got on with the job.

Later on, I had to put someone in 'the rattle,' as disciplinary proceedings were more commonly known. AB H. was nicknamed Redeye for his constantly tired-looking appearance. Others often found him asleep when he should have been on watch or working, and getting him out of his bunk in the mornings was an ongoing struggle. He would peer at you through red-rimmed eyes, muttering, “Okay, I’ll be there in a minute,” and then fall asleep as soon as your back was turned. He was often late or absent from duty, and was frequently in trouble.

One morning, Redeye disappeared from his part of ship, where he ought to have been at work, so I went in search of him. Skiving was something we all did, up to a point. But to my amazement, I found him tucked up in his bunk asleep. I couldn’t ignore this, so I started the disciplinary wheels in motion. Redeye’s offense surprised no one, and he didn't get much sympathy. More surprisingly, though, instead of receiving yet another minor punishment, the Navy discharged him with SNLR - services no longer required. Perhaps it did him a favour in the long run. I hope so, though it wasn't something that troubled me too much at the time.

Generally, discipline wasn't a problem. But the radar plotter's mess had a handful of troublemakers. Whilst most of us were amiable idiots when drunk, these lads could be aggressive troublemakers.

One voyage took us to Loch Ewe in the western highlands of Scotland. There was little to do off duty except to find the nearest hotel and drink. As usual, I drank quite a bit. At the end of the night I staggered off down some godforsaken country lane, heading towards the jetty. Then fortune smiled on me, and I saw a car with a light on top, which I thought could only have been a taxi.

"Take me to the warship please," I said to one of the two drivers. It was only when we arrived and the men refused the fare that I noticed through drink-fuddled vision that I'd been in a police car.

Getting out of the 'taxi,' I saw some of the radar plotters living up to the ship's motto: *Timeunt Danaeides* - 'Fear those belonging to Danac.' Fists flew, and having neither the ability nor the inclination to stop it, I settled for a ringside seat until it was over.

The next bout of trouble couldn't be ignored, though. One evening, I was quartermaster in charge of the gangway, during the first watch, whilst the libertymen were coming back from their run ashore. Two of the radar plotters came back on board, clearly drunk. They chatted amicably to me and then staggered out of sight down a hatchway. The next thing I heard was the duty PO shouting, "No, Tomo!" Immediately after came the sound of a blow as Tomo thumped him on the nose.

Tomo and his oppo spent the rest of the night locked up down the tiller flat. A few days later they were put on a charge, and I had to stand as a witness. I stated that they weren't causing any trouble whilst they were on the gangway with me. However, I wasn't sympathetic when T. was given a discharge from the RN via an unpleasant stay in the Royal Naval Detention Quarters in Portsmouth dockyard.

Trouble and fighting wasn't commonplace on HMS Danae, and it was a welcome return to normality when we heard we were going to Gibraltar. I'd already been there on HMS Grenville, and mightily impressed I was, too, especially by the Rock of Gibraltar. The Army took us on a guided tour of the underground facilities hidden deep inside the massive limestone promontory for protection from aerial bombardment.

The Army also took us to see the apes which live higher up on the outside slopes of the Rock. Legend has it, that if the apes leave the Rock, so will the British. Not surprisingly, someone was employed to keep an eye on them. This chap offered to get an ape to sit on our shoulders for photographs. Most of us kept a wary distance. But one of the artificers, Tiffie, persuaded the ape-keeper to get the ape to sit on his head. Then, to the amusement of the rest of us, the ape shit over Tiffie's head.

Whilst we were in Gibraltar, someone had the bright idea of trying for an entry in the *Guinness Book of Records* for the world's biggest tug of war. It was a match between the Plymouth- and

Portsmouth-based ships. Ever keen to avoid work, I volunteered for the three hundred strong Plymouth team.

We used a massive multi-plait towing hawser, strong enough to tow another warship. Rope stretches under tension; we all knew this, but no one predicted just how far or how fast it would contract again.

We picked up the rope for the first pull, but when the rope was dropped, it contracted at breakneck speed, whipping the massive steel shackles on the end around in the air, smashing into some of the lads. They hit one man on the head, sending him to hospital with life-threatening injuries, and hurt a few others quite badly. I can't remember who won the tug of war, but after that we abandoned the record-breaking attempt.

The tug-of-war was an unfortunate and isolated accident. I was more likely to injure myself through drunken behaviour. Once, I came back after a night ashore in Portsmouth and staggered on board the wrong ship. It was another Leander class frigate, like HMS Danae, but it was undergoing major refit and lots of the deck was missing. I tottered around the steel frames that supported the now-missing deck, looking for my bunk, swaying from side to side over the sheer drop until rescued by the quartermaster.

HMS Danae was sent to join the Standing Naval Force Atlantic, or Stanavforlant for short. This was a NATO-tasked squadron, made up of ships from NATO countries. There was a US destroyer, USS Coontz, and a Canadian frigate, initially HMCS Athabaskan and then HMCS Assinaboine. The squadron also had Dutch and German frigates, plus a Portuguese warship that appeared briefly on the horizon one day and then disappeared just as quickly, not to be seen again.

Predictably, we were deployed in the North Atlantic, with visits to Bermuda, Puerto Rico, the USA, and Canada. One day, a note appeared on daily orders inviting volunteers to spend a week on board one of the other ships in the squadron. To my surprise, this didn't prove to be very popular. Seeing it as a welcome break from routine cleaning, painting, and polishing - activities that were losing their shine, if you'll forgive the pun - I put my name down.

So off I went to the US destroyer, where I was completely ignored by officialdom, and spent a week doing nothing. I had a great break, unlike the American sailor who took my place onboard HMS Danae. He worked part of ship and watchkeeping and probably wished he'd never bothered.

My next opportunity to promote cross-cultural nautical awareness came with a week onboard the Dutch frigate. This time our gunnery officer was also part of the exchange. A Dutch officer took us both on a tour of the ship. I looked at the gunnery officer and thought, *This time I'm not going to be able to skive.* Then, seeming to sense my thoughts, this splendid man sent me on some spurious task, and I didn't see him again for a week.

The food onboard the Dutch frigate was prepared by Indonesian cooks. It seemed to be endless varieties of stew, with what appeared to be fish eyes staring out of it, plus rationed chips. But the scran was compensated for by the unlimited beer for sale, unlike our ration of three cans a day. Predictably, I drank horrible quantities of booze whilst avoiding work. I returned to HMS Danae a week later, skint but happy.

After visiting various ports in the USA, the squadron sailed north to Halifax in Nova Scotia. This is where I met Sheila. The saying goes that a 'sailor has a girl in every port.' This is much exaggerated - certainly so in my case.

Sheila asked me to dance at a disco in the Drill Hall in Halifax. To cut a long story short, we spent a couple of weeks cementing Anglo-Canadian relations, whilst her husband worked with a different kind of cement, building the Olympic Stadium in Montreal. Sheila and I weren't in love. We didn't know each other long enough for that. She was lonely and in need of warmth and affection, and I was starved of female company. She made me laugh, too, especially when we went into a nice hotel and ordered a pot of tea. I asked if she would pour. She refused in embarrassment, convinced that, being English, I would insist on tea being poured in some very genteel English way. As the relationship progressed, she began having twinges of conscience, but I wasn't the least bit concerned that she was married. I knew it wasn't going anywhere, though I was a bit sad when I had to say goodbye.

When our turn of duty with Stanavforlant was completed, we sailed home. I spent most of my time in Portsmouth dockyard painting and cleaning. Eventually, the tedium blunted my earlier enthusiasm for a lifetime at sea, and I applied for premature voluntary release (PVR).

Premature voluntary release was a new scheme, allowing me to leave the Navy in eighteen months time in return for a cut in pay. It was a big decision. Despite some disciplinary hiccups, I'd done well to be promoted so early, and I could expect further promotion in due course. My divisional officer had suggested applying for the upper yardman scheme for training to be commissioned as an officer. The first step was studying for some GCE O levels, which I thought of as akin to rocket science. I applied to the Education Office in Naval Barracks for a correspondence course. But, foolishly, I gave up after only a few weeks: Lieutenant L had gone through all this himself years earlier, and it's a great shame that I didn't stick with it and follow his example.

Lieutenant L. had been commissioned from the lower deck. He was a good friend and mentor to me. Indeed, he'd given me my one and only experience of commanding one of Her Majesty's warships at sea. One night, during the middle watch, he was on the bridge as officer of the watch, and I was bridge messenger. He needed to use the heads and disappeared, telling me to "keep an eye on things."

Then a contact report came in from the radar operator in the ops room: the starboard lookout reported a light visible, and the wheelhouse asked permission to change the helmsman. I'd been at sea long enough to deal with the routine, so I gave the wheelhouse permission to change the helmsman and acknowledged the lookout's report. If another officer had happened to come onto the bridge, Lieutenant L. would have probably ended up in deep shit.

Fortunately, that didn't happen. He returned, and my brief spell of command was over.

My main job was seamanship, but I had a sub-specialisation as a gunner. Later, some Whitehall warrior with an eye to public relations changed *gunner* to *missileman*. But if anyone supposes that we constantly (or even frequently) fired any of the ship's weapon systems, they'll be as disappointed as I used to be. We practised, we drilled, but we very rarely saw live ammunition. The reason is probably easy to guess: money. High explosive shells were expensive, and missiles cost a mint.

The Seacat ship to air anti-aircraft missile system was being superseded by newer systems like Seawolf, with more sophisticated electronic guidance systems. But Seacat's relative simplicity made it an exciting bit of kit to fire. The aimer steers the missile via radio control, whilst tracking the target through an optical sight. So the ship's main radar finds the target aircraft at long range. The ops room indicates the target to the Seacat control room. The control room launches the missile into the aimer's field of view, and the aimer steers it to the target. Easy!

The missile director was a large, rotating bin-shaped object with a narrow beam radar on the side. Inside the director was the most important bit of kit: me. I would climb in through a door in the side and stand on a platform, looking through a binocular sight linked to the radar. A small thumb control next to the sight controlled the missile in flight. Move the control up, and the missile flew higher; move it left, and the missile flew left, and so on. Simple in theory, but challenging in practice with a sub-sonic missile.

Being the big cheese in this system earned me a shiny gold rocket badge on my No1 uniform. I would tell gullible civilians that I was a trainee astronaut. As a further aside, one of the crew, Jan Harmer, was an ex-submariner. He wore the submarine service badge of two dolphins either side of a crown. He would tell the even more gullible that this was the badge of the Queen's dolphin trainer.

But back to matters ballistic. The platform inside the director could be raised or lowered to suit the height of the operator. Or at least it had been designed to; some bonehead had welded an electrical box in the way. This left the platform permanently stuck at a level suited to an American basketball player rather than a five-foot, four-inch maritime midget like me. I had to wedge my feet on the sides of the director to reach the sight, and then jump down to the platform to operate the foot switches.

My big day eventually came. The master gunner summoned me and relayed that I was going to fire a couple of live missiles. My excitement was only slightly diminished when I discovered they would have cheaper inert warheads; proper warheads had a proximity fuse and forty pounds of high explosive, surrounded by hundreds of metal rods designed to fragment, causing lethal damage to aircraft and pilot.

The target aircraft didn't have a pilot, but was launched and controlled from another ship a few miles away. So, given the lack of a warhead and the small size of the pilotless aircraft, my chances of actually shooting it down were minimal. But no matter, I was playing with some very expensive toys at the taxpayer's expense.

I could hear the Seacat controller through my headphones, acknowledging the target indication from the ops room. The order

"Seacat salvos" boomed into my left ear. The launcher and director trained to port, aiming at the tiny black dot that was the attacking aircraft. The captain's voice came over my headset with, "Engage," the command permission to open fire.

I shouted, "Target!" This meant I could see the rapidly approaching aircraft well enough to fly the missile. As the aircraft came into range, the controller said, "Shoot!" and I felt a buzz of adrenaline as three electronic bleeps warned me of missile launch.

With an ear-splitting roar, the missile launched up into the sky. It flew wildly for a couple of seconds before I gathered it into the crosshairs of my sight, which were lined up on the target. Using subtle control movements, I brought the missile up to the aircraft, where the fuse of a live warhead would have exploded, blasting lethal fragments of steel into the target. Then, seconds later, the missile's motor burnt out and it fell spiralling into the sea. It was great fun, despite not having been able to destroy the target. Unfortunately, I only got to fire one more missile, defence budget restrictions being more important than effective defence training. But, as always, there was soon something else to get excited about and soon after, HMS Danae was involved in the making of a television series.

I'd already had one little brush with celluloid onboard HMS Grenville. A film crew had come aboard to make a documentary film starring Kenneth Griffith called *The Man on the Rock*. It was some arty, modern day depiction of Napoleon's journey into exile, hence the use of a modern warship and a cast in modern uniform. No doubt this kept the budget under control, early-nineteenth-century warships being as rare as rocking horse shit. None of this concerned me, though. I happily volunteered as an extra, marching Napoleon back and forth across the quarterdeck. Anything for a break in routine or a skive from work. Later, I heard that the film was very popular in the USA and especially California, where it was much admired by film director Stanley Kubrick.

My next 'role' came when HMS Danae was in harbour filming scenes for the television series *Warship*. As usual, the lads showed little interest for anything that involved dressing up in No1 uniform. No such inhibition stopped yours truly. I happily played the part of bosun's mate, blowing the bosun's call (whistle) for the daily ceremony of sunset, when the ensign was lowered. (Incidentally, I never got to see any of this myself, so if anyone out there has copies, I'd be eternally grateful . . .)

With the film crew aboard, we sailed on to Torbay, where they brought potted palm trees onto the beach and used special lenses to make a dull day look sunny, creating the appearance of the Far East. I wasn't involved this time - perhaps just as well, as I'd already got to the stage of offering advice to the film crew.

Unlike me, the Royal Marine officer in command of the ship's marine detachment refused any involvement with the film crew. He earned my admiration when he steadfastly refused to lend his Sam Browne belt to the actor playing the part of a Marine officer. The belt being his own property, he was perfectly entitled to do so, but it took a degree of moral fibre to refuse the urging of the captain, who is obeyed with God-like awe onboard a warship.

One day I was summoned to the regulating office. Wondering what I might have done, I reported and was presented with a draft chit. A few weeks later, I found myself in the Royal Naval Barracks in Stonehouse, Plymouth.

So there I was, seven years on, coming to the end of my seagoing career. The fifteen-year-old boy seaman was now a leading seaman, in charge of a section of the barrack guard. One thing that hadn't changed, however, was my height. I was still five feet and four inches tall, but after years of good food and too much falling down water, I had a big fat beer belly. And I was losing motivation, getting bored, and beginning to think of a new career.

The Royal Navy itself had gone through lots of changes. New ships were coming into service. New uniforms were being brought in, in an effort to update Jack's appearance. Personally, I preferred the traditional uniform. One long-overdue improvement was better accommodation ashore. Some of the messing that I'd experienced as a junior seaman in Portsmouth barracks, whilst HMS Grenville was in refit, literally hadn't changed since Queen Victoria had sat on the throne. Now, as a killick, I actually had my own room. It was tiny, and I couldn't lock the door, but compared to a warship's messdeck, it was luxurious.

Not long after this, I had my twenty-second birthday. Aside from getting stupidly drunk, I was awarded my first stripe for good conduct (generally referred to as undetected crime).

Being in barracks was fine - decent accommodation, easy access to the delights of Union Street - and I wasn't exactly worked to death. But it was boring, so I volunteered for service in Northern Ireland. Then, a few weeks later, I received a draft chit to report to the Naval Liaison Officer Northern Ireland.

Chapter Ten

-

On 13 February 1977, I arrived at Moscow Camp, near Hollywood, on the outskirts of Belfast. It was run by the Royal Corps of Transport; why it was called Moscow, I'll never know. The camp was at the end of a long road that ran from the docks in Belfast to the camp and was insulated from Hollywood by marshes.

I'd arrived expecting some typical barrack job. So I was pleasantly surprised, but a little nervous, when I was told to report to the Intelligence Cell. Visions of being some lower deck James Bond were soon quashed. But it was a very good posting, with an informal but efficient work-hard-and-play-hard ethos.

The officer commanding the intelligence cell was Lieutenant Roland G., RM. He was a nice guy who treated his staff well, and I was pleased to hear recently that he's now a lieutenant colonel. There were three RM sergeants: Dave J., Ernie H., and Tom I. Later on we were joined by (Big) Spike K. These NCOs were all ten or fifteen years older than me, and ten times fitter, too.

Seven years of overeating and heavy drinking with little real fitness training hadn't done my waistline any good. But, encouraged by the bootnecks, I put myself on a diet, went to the sauna and gym every day, and started running. It was fantastic - I'd discovered fitness. The weight fell off me, I looked and felt much better, and my success rate at the camp dance every Saturday increased exponentially.

At the weekend, both the NAAFI bar and the RCT corporal's mess held discos. Young ladies arrived in the back of Bedford four-ton trucks. They were security-vetted and, no doubt, from a Protestant background. They were free to range between either disco at whim. It wasn't sophisticated nightlife; it certainly wasn't representative of Ulster's ethnic and cultural diversity. But we didn't give a bollocks, and everyone enjoyed themselves.

There was an old portakabin near the vehicle park, where a couple of Pakistanis sold high-cholesterol greaseburgers to hungry squaddies. The lads took their girlfriends there en route in order to cement military/civilian relations in an empty vehicle. Sadly, most of these liaisons were frustrated by the patrol posted to keep the civvies in the bar and NAAFI area. It wasn't anything moral, just a security precaution; everyone agreed in principle, but tried to ignore it in practice, when the blood flowed from the brain to certain other regions.

The Intelligence Cell was a small unit with restricted access, and we were left to our own devices. We were concerned with stopping the flow of illegal weapons and explosives into Northern Ireland. In reality, we were a little cog in a big wheel. We didn't have any assets (agents) in the field, and any intelligence we received was generally second hand. Nonetheless, we did what we could, and little that it was, I thoroughly enjoyed it. We maintained patrols using wooden-hulled Ton class minesweepers, which were attached to us on short tours of duty.

The minesweepers stopped and boarded merchant vessels bound for Northern Ireland. The boarding parties were led by one of our RM sergeants whose codename was Searider. They were privy to all the latest intelligence, such as which PIRA terrorists were involved with shipping and so on.

My job was pretty straightforward. I collated information and updated files with the latest intelligence. We didn't have computers; everything was written or typed and kept in filing cabinets. The Seariders went out to the minesweepers and directed the boarding parties and searches, and the boss organised and liaised. Occasionally, we were involved with operations on Carlingford Lough, on the border between Ulster and the Republic of Ireland. It all sounds simple, but try searching a supertanker. The sheer size makes it nigh impossible to find much, unless you are either very lucky or you receive good intelligence.

At some point, someone came up with the bright idea of using a submarine to covertly monitor suspect vessels, such as the Bally boats. These were small scruffy merchant ships, belonging to a shipping company with IRA links.

Captain G., Sergeant I., and I were dispatched to Scotland to try it out. We flew to the naval base at Rosyth in a Sea King helicopter, and made our way to the big Intelligence Cell. The boss gave a briefing before returning to Moscow Camp. He introduced Tom to the gathering of ops and intelligence officers. Then he turned to face me. "This is L/S Widders, he's one of our team," he said in a strong voice that didn't invite criticism. The looks from the assembled intelligence officers made it clear that they weren't used to junior ratings being part of the setup, so I didn't waste any words. Instead, in time-honoured naval tradition, I wandered around their well-stocked little empire to see what I could pinch.

After the briefings, Tom and I went down to the jetty to the submarine. It was an 'O' boat, one of a class whose names all began with the letter O. I walked across the brow and passed through an open hatch into the submarine's main passageway. The coxswain stood there and looked at me. He assumed I was a new crewmember and pointed towards what looked to me like an empty bookcase. "Here's your bunk," he said, laughing at the look of disbelief on my face. I swiftly disillusioned him, and he directed me to the seaman's mess and something marginally more comfortable.

Even as an experienced seaman, being on a submarine was something of a novelty, and not one that I'd care to repeat. A frigate isn't spacious, but compared to a submarine, it's five-star. I did manage to find a nicer heads (toilet) than the one the other seamen were using. It seemed just a bit more spacious and clean, but eventually I realised it was the captain's, so I wisely decided not to push my special passenger status by using it again.

We spent the next couple of days submerged off the coast of Ireland, quietly watching fishing boats and merchant vessels through the periscope. But with hundreds of miles of coastline, the odds of seeing some clandestine activity were not good. It clearly wasn't proving to be worthwhile, and the future routine use of subs for surveillance was later quietly dropped.

While we were on the sub, the yeoman back at NLONI sent us the football results by coded signal; he also informed us that our time on the submarine was drawing to a close. The following day at dawn, we surfaced. Tom and I emerged through the hatch and climbed up through the conning tower. Water streamed off the metalwork, and the light of the dawn illuminated the foam blowing off the green, wind-flecked waves. We could hear the *wap wap* sound of a helicopter's rotors as it approached. The crewman leant out of the side door, ready to guide the winch wire down to us. I was winched up, followed by Tom, and we flew off as the submarine receded in the distance.

Back at camp, life resumed its usual round of work and play. Work wasn't too arduous. Much of it was routine paper shuffling, in which I was helped by my oppo, Eddie W., who had recently joined us. The boss continued his unsuccessful attempts to create an aura of eccentricity. He'd sit underneath his desk, muttering to himself, whilst checking through the safe's contents of secret papers.

His occasional efforts at eccentricity were tongue in cheek and fooled no one. He was a nice guy and a good boss of our tight knit team. He occasionally made coffee for everyone. It was truly awful, and eventually we banned his efforts at democracy and just made it ourselves.

I was happy at NLONI and didn't relish leaving at the end of my six-month tour. But the boss applied to drafty and had it extended to a year. I was chuffed with that, as I felt I was doing something worthwhile, especially compared to my previous work on frigates, where I'd become to feel something of a seagoing painter and decorator.

1977 was the year of the Queen's silver jubilee, and Her Majesty decided to come out and pay the good folk of Northern Ireland a visit. It was well deserved, too, as a significant proportion of the populace just wanted to get on with their lives in peace and didn't support terrorists of whatever hue.

I was given the job of coxswain on one of the launches, ferrying guests out to the many receptions held onboard the Royal Yacht Britannia. We borrowed a splendid twin diesel launch from the Flag Officer Scotland. Intelligence duties forgotten, I practised handling her in Belfast docks and harbour. Another borrowed launch appeared, skippered by a fat git who shall remain anonymous, and instigated a game of high-speed chicken through the docks. The result was the near destruction of a radar set being fitted to a minesweeper, which rocked violently in our combined wake, causing the electricians to drop the radar set. A serious bollocking resulted, but what the hell, it wasn't the first one, and it certainly wasn't going to be the last.

Britannia anchored off Bangor on the Ards peninsula. I sailed the launch down there and spent the day ferrying VIPs out to the yacht. One of our sergeants was invited to a reception. On his return trip, I let Dave have a go at steering the launch, and he amused me by telling me about the reception: "Met the Duke of Edinburgh, who looked at me, snorted, and said, 'Another bloody Royal Marine.'"

Earlier in the day, a small, wooden, beautifully varnished fishing boat had joined us, manned by uniformed ratings from the local Royal Naval Reserve establishment. This surreal-looking vessel attracted the attention of one of the Royal Ulster Constabulary's patrol boats, which came alongside me.

"What the hell's that?" asked an RUC sergeant in a heavy Ulster accent.

Always keen to use what I fondly imagined was my native Scouse wit, I replied, "It's the Royal Fish Barge." To my surprise, they believed me.

The day came to an end, and the launch was lifted out of the water by crane and placed on the back of a giant trailer to be transported back to Scotland. Meanwhile, I was busy chatting up a Royal Naval Reserve Wren at the reception laid on for the boat's crews.

Being one of a small detachment of sailors based in a large Army camp had advantages. One of them was the buying power of duty-free Navy cigarettes. Though I didn't smoke, plenty of the squaddies did, and I became adept at bargaining for useful items of kit from their stores. The boss nicknamed me King Rat after a character in a James Clavell novel, a POW in a Jap prison camp who was renowned for his scrounging skills.

Whenever shuffling paper threatened to be too much tedium, something would happen to brighten life up. When I went into Belfast it was usually in civvies, and my fairly long hair helping me to blend in and not look military. Occasionally I had to don flak jacket and rifle, usually on some undemanding escort duty well away from any of the 'hard' areas. Like all servicemen in Northern Ireland, I carried the infamous yellow card detailing the rules of engagement. A lot of nonsense has been written and spoken about this card. It laid out the conditions under which you were able to open fire. Basically, you could shoot if you were fired upon or were about to be fired upon. You only had to shout a warning if it was practicable; the yellow card wasn't as restrictive as it was made out to be.

One thing that surprised me was the amount of ammunition carried on urban street patrols. One of the squaddies told me they could only carry three rounds, which seemed ridiculously conservative to me. So, being a firm believer in the old maxim that you can never have too much ammunition, I always had a minimum of two full magazines - forty rounds - for my rifle.

Ironically, the only time I ever really needed any firepower, I didn't have it. I'd been used to having fairly long hair and wandering freely around Belfast in civvies, though avoiding the worst hard-line republican areas. Not long before leaving Ireland, I had my hair cut, ready for the delights of barracks in Plymouth. I then thoughtlessly walked into a republican bar I'd sometimes visited. The barman walked past me to collect some beer glasses. "Get the fuck out outta here," he mouthed quietly at me. I noticed some guys making towards me. The look in their hard, brutalised eyes said it all. I'd been spotted as a member of the security forces and was about to be attacked, or maybe snatched. One guy ran to block the exit, but he wasn't quick enough. I dropped my pint and legged it out the door faster than hot shit off a shiny shovel. I was unarmed, so I broke the land speed record getting out of the area. I was able to laugh about it afterwards, but at the time it was a bit tense.

When a minesweeper was on station, one of our sergeants was carried onboard to advise and lead the search parties. It wasn't really my job, but on occasion I was sent out to help. I went out to one of the minesweepers with an Army dog handler and his Labrador sniffer dog. Once in harness, he went off searching without any need of encouragement. The handler and I just wandered around behind him and nosed around for anything else of interest.

It was tiring work for the dog, so we asked to be set ashore to give him some exercise - a bit of canine R&R. Dressed in aircrew survival suits, and with a lifejacket on the dog, we headed for the beach in a fast Gemini dinghy. As we were still in Belfast Lough, we chose to land in familiar territory, near Hollywood, which was one of the safer areas. Nonetheless, we were well armed with SLR assault rifles and plenty of ammunition.

The Gemini hit the beach and we jumped out. We charged through the mild surf, doing our best John Wayne impressions, to the surprise of some early morning walkers. Dog, dog handler, and myself enjoyed a good walk ashore. Then we went back to the Gemini and made a fast passage across Belfast Lough to the waiting minesweeper.

A few days later, Tom and I were in the Customs and Excise Office at Portrush. We received a message to come back to base to act as escort and take a prisoner to England. He was a sailor who had been AWOL and was being returned to Portsmouth for trial. His most probable prospect wasn't enviable - a spell in the Royal Naval Detention Quarters in Portsmouth dockyard. But it was good news for Tom, who lived near Exmouth and would have a chance to get home and see his wife.

The flight took us to Exeter, where a crusher (naval policeman) met us and drove us to Plymouth. The crusher dropped Tom off on the A38, where he could thumb a lift home. That left the crusher and me to escort the prisoner, who wasn't causing any trouble. On arrival, we gave him over to the tender care of the duty regulating petty officer, who then turned to me and said, "Where would you like a lift to?" The novel result was me being taken *to* Union Street in a patrol van, where I sank a few beers before getting the train to Newton Abbot to visit my mother. I tried to visit her as often as possible, and we remained very close. She was still proud that I was serving in the Navy, though she must have worried about my heavy drinking. Life was tough as ever for her, bringing up my sister on a very limited income. I could have helped more, especially if I had directed more of my income towards my family and less over the bar. But drinkers are the last ones to see the problem. Yet again I was on the train heading home and wasting my money on overpriced British Rail canned beer.

I'd got so many trains over the years that I felt I knew the timetables back to front. But I got it badly wrong once. Nearly all trains travelling from Exeter to Plymouth stopped at Newton Abbot. I didn't check this one, however, and it one whizzed through the station without stopping and then slowed down near the Torquay Road. Seeing my chance, I opened the door and jumped out, clutching my pusser's grip (holdall). I landed on the embankment as the train picked up speed, and an oppo closed the door behind me. I jumped over the fence and walked into Newton Abbott, bruised but relieved. As always, it was nice to see my family. My sister was still living at home and my mom was delighted to see me and even more delighted to show me the little vegetable garden she'd starting growing behind the house.

When my weekend leave was over, I met Tom in Liverpool. We were booked on to the Belfast ferry, a floating Wild West town with drunken shenanigans all over the place. A few days after getting back to camp, we were both summoned to the Jimmy's (first lieutenant) office where Tom got a rocket for leaving the prisoner before reaching Plymouth. The crusher had made a complaint, which seemed a bit rough, as he had agreed at the time. However, that's life in the services.

My time in the RN was drawing to an end; my application for the new premature voluntary release scheme had been successful. The captain was keen to see me stay on, so he sent for me to have a chat. He wasn't such a remote figure as you'd imagine the captain of a warship. I'd often spoken with him during meetings, like the recent one in the Intelligence Cell, where the possibility of us abseiling down from a helicopter onto the stern of suspect merchant ships was discussed - and abandoned.

He said, "Well, Widders, if you sign on, I'll do my best to get you the draft of your choice. What about the Royal Yacht Britannia?"

"Very tempting, sir, but no thank you," I replied. I knew that one way or another, it would be back to the old routine of painting and cleaning, and I didn't relish that any more.

Just before Christmas 1977, I was sent on leave with orders to report to HMS Drake, the Naval Barracks, in January. I was in the Cider Bar on East Street, chatting to an old shipmate who lived in Newton Abbot. He had a suggestion; being a master-at-arms, he knew how to fiddle my leave record card. So we unsealed the envelope and he altered it to show that I was due for fourteen days leave that hadn't been taken yet.

After the usual drunken stay in Newton, I reported to the regulating office in Drake Barracks, Plymouth.

“Think I might be due a spot of leave, RPO,” I said, in my best innocent tone.

"So you are, lad," he said, after looking at my leave card. Then he gave me a fourteen-day pass, and I headed back to Newton Abbot.

When I returned to barracks, I was put to work with the buffer's party for a couple of weeks before going to Portsmouth to do a resettlement course. I did motor mechanics and spent four weeks totally mystified, trying to understand the workings of the internal combustion engine. Despite my lack of talent, I received a handsome certificate extolling my many mechanical virtues - as did everyone else.

After the course, I was sent back to Plymouth to be discharged and hand my kit in. I walked through the barrack gates for the last time, never to wear the Queen's uniform again. Or so I thought.

Chapter Eleven

The thrill of not being told what to do and when to do it soon worn off A few days spent standing in the Cider Bar on East Street started to knock a hole in my last fortnightly Navy pay, and it was also boring sitting around doing nothing, missing my mates and the camaraderie. So I went to the job centre to find a job. I had the City and Guilds certificate that I'd been given in the Navy's recent drive to have its training recognised in civvy street. I also felt that I was a proven leader with a whole range of skills and experience. Newton Abbot's spotty-faced dole clerk clearly thought differently.

"What was your last job?" asked spotty youth.

"Naval Intelligence," I replied nonchalantly, expecting him to be impressed. He looked at me with quiet disbelief.

"Might be some labouring work," hc said.

I went to see my Uncle Percy. He was working for Centrax, at Heathfield near Newton Abbot, and he had a word with the foreman. After a brief interview, I was given a job as a radial drill operator. I started on the night shift, and an ex-Marine chargehand showed me how to operate the huge drills, making axle parts for heavy goods vehicles. It was unbelievably boring. The one consolation was that the pay was good. It was even better when I stumbled onto my own method of counting the number of parts I drilled.

The system was simple, really. A piece might be timed, for example, at three minutes each. Do more than twenty in one hour, and you would earn a bonus payment. This increased according to the percentage over target you achieved. To make things easier for new employees, you could be clocked as 'under training' and paid a set bonus, regardless of how many - or how few - pieces per hour you drilled.

With each new job, I would clock as under training for a few hours and then clock at normal rates to try to earn a high bonus. What I didn’t realise initially was that the parts drilled whilst under training had to be counted separately. Instead, I counted the work done under training in the total count for bonus. Confused? So was

I. But until someone realised what was happening, my apparent hourly work rate was phenomenal, and I earned a bloody fortune.

Despite the money, drilling holes in axle parts was so boring that I resigned. Pontins were looking for staff, so I sent off an application. A few days later, whilst sleeping off the effects of a Sunday lunchtime visit to the Cider Bar, there was a knock at the door of my mother's house in Margaret Road, Kingsteignton. It was PC Coles, the village bobby. He'd been sent by his ex-policeman pal at Pontin's with a message for me to attend an interview in Brixham the next day.

I started work the following day as bar security officer and night patrolman. The wages were derisory. But food, and my own little wooden chalet, was free. Work started in the evening when the bar opened. My diminutive stature surprised quite a few people. One evening, one of the bar staff walked up to me and said quietly, "Hey, Rob. We've been told you're a Kung Fu expert—is that true?"

"I'm certainly not," I answered, and couldn't help laughing at the thought. The real reason for the lack of lack of trouble was simply that everyone was there to have a good time. The hardest battle was convincing the bar staff that I wasn't a management spy, so that I could get the same unofficial bar discount as the rest of the staff. When the bar closed, I had to do the occasional patrol of the camp and be available in reception until 0600 the next morning.

Life settled into a pleasant routine. Each evening I would have a few drinks whilst keeping an eye on the bar. After the bar closed, I would open up the kitchens and have a midnight meal with few other staff members; I had all the camp's keys, so I made use of them.

Every week, a new set of holidaymakers arrived. There were plenty of girls around, so, being a normal young man, I met a few; enough said. However, the Head of Entertainment was of a different persuasion. His name was Reg Lane, otherwise known by his stage name, Angel. Unfortunately, he took an obvious liking to me, though it was never a problem. He offered to give me a Bluecoat's job at a camp in the Channel Islands when this one closed. Given my total lack of talent or potential as an entertainer, it wasn‘t hard to spot the ulterior motive.

My job finished at the end of the holiday season. I spent a few days with my mother in Kingsteignton, and then went to Southampton to meet the people with whom I was going to Africa. Before leaving the Navy, I'd spent time chatting with an oppo who used to spend his leaves travelling and backpacking. He told me about a magazine for overland travellers, and I felt inspired to try something adventurous myself. I got in touch with Corinne and Jane via the magazine. Corinne worked in a bar and Jane worked for a ferry company. Both girls lived in Southampton, and they were looking for someone to share the expenses of an overland trip across the Sahara and then through west and central Africa.

I paid Jane and Corinne a third share for a Land Rover. There was another vehicle, too, crewed by Derrick and a couple, Pete and Helen. They all knew each other from previous trips. I was a newcomer, and we all had to make a decision about how well I would fit in on the basis of a couple of meetings. It was a gamble.

Everything started off well enough. We took the Townsend-Thoreson ferry to France. Jane used to work on board at the reception, where, amongst other things, they allocated sleeping couchettes. She told us that one day a guy came up to her and asked to "book a courgette"; made me laugh, anyway.

We drove through France and across the Alps. The mountains were picture-postcard-pretty in places, with distant snowy peaks and clear blue lakes. One morning I clambered down a rock and scree covered slope. I bathed in a river that poured in torrents down the ravine, next to the road. The water was more bloody cold than I could ever have imagined, so I got out quickly and got on with the journey

It was pretty uneventful until we approached Turin. It was late in the evening, so we camped in a field. It was misty, and we couldn't see much. The next morning, we woke to discover that we were in someone's front garden. Packing up at breakneck speed, we continued onwards, taking the ferry to Sicily and then taking another ferry to Tunis. This was where the cracks started to appear.

Derrick was doing the maintenance of both vehicles and accused us of using him. We then met a guy who was going to cross the Sahara on a motorbike. He asked if he could travel with us, and Derrick and the couple falsely accused us of planning to ditch them. It all blew up into a big row. I wasn't used to all this tedious civilian crap but tried my best to be positive in discussion. Eventually the cracks were papered over, and we continued with the trip.

We passed by the oil fields at Hassi Massouad and crossed the border into Algeria. The desert was spectacular on the Tassili n'Ajjer Plateau, en route to the tiny mountain oasis of Djanet. Why they had a customs post in the middle of the desert, totally removed from any border, was a mystery to me. But the customs officers acted like the circus had come to town—they were thrilled with our arrival. It must have been a boring life for them, and I guess they didn't see many European girls. They drooled over Jane and Corinne, and I had to keep a chaperone-like presence at all times.

It was close to the Muslim religious festival of Eid, so they persuaded us to stay as their guests at the customs house. They obtained a sheep from somewhere, probably at great cost, as sheep weren't exactly common in the middle of the Sahara desert. The poor creature was tethered in the yard of the customs house until the morning of the feast, when it disappeared. In the evening it appeared again; it was lying on its back in a bed of rice, legs raised in the air. My companions all declared themselves vegetarians—liars. I sat there, staring at an emaciated mass of skin and bones. It looked as if it had died of starvation rather than being butchered. The customs officers sat back, waiting for me, the honoured guest, to eat first. At least they didn't present the eyeballs, which would have been beyond me, regardless of courtesy. So I desperately hacked around for five minutes, looking for some meat amongst the sinew and gristle, until I could persuade the customs officers that I'd had enough.

Eventually, we escaped from the hospitality of the *douane,* or customs, and continued our desert journey. We visited old, atmospheric French Foreign Legion forts and caves with prehistoric rock art. In Tammanrasset, we briefly rejoined a tarmac road for a drive into the dusty, bustling oasis town. After resting up for a few days, we headed south on the road to Niger.

We drove down the dirt road, full of excitement and glad to be on the road at last. Then Corinne said the ominous words, "Does anyone hear a knockin' sound coming from the engine?" We agreed that it was probably nothing much and kept going. But the noise worsened, and we signalled the other vehicle to stop.

Derrick was the only one of the group with any real automotive knowledge. He walked over and listened to the engine. He looked gloomy, saying, "That sounds serious - best we tow you back to Tam."

We came to rest outside the mud-walled camping site with its reed *zaribas* (huts). The problem was a broken crankshaft, which was a nightmare to sort out in socialist Algeria, which was suffering from a distinct lack of Land Rover spare parts.

For the next few weeks, we tried various agencies, who all promised to obtain a crankshaft from Algiers. The boredom started to get to us all. We'd read the two or three books we had between us, so one day we crammed into the other Rover and headed to Assekrem. We stayed overnight at the refuge, which was built around 1910 by the French missionary Charles de Foucauld. It was a truly spectacular place. All around, arid rocky peaks rose up nine thousand feet. I looked up at hidden plateaus and fancifully imagined a lost secret oasis. This was all very nice, but when we got back to Tam, we still lacked a crankshaft.

Sitting around for six weeks strained already tenuous friendships. I decided not to waste more time sitting in the middle of the Sahara staring at a broken Land Rover. So I booked a flight to Algiers. I flew on December 25, on an aeroplane like an Arab bus, with passengers carrying just about everything except goats.

It was nice to be back in Devon. But I was skint, so I had to get on and do something. I visited the Royal Marines recruiting office in Exeter. They regretted to inform me that I was too short to join the Marines. The minimum height was five foot, five inches, and I was an inch short. So the answer seemed obvious: I went to the recruiting office in Torquay and joined the Army.

Part Two: The Army

Chapter Twelve

Staff Sergeant Mick Davy interviewed me for the Army.

"I'm interested in joining the Parachute Regiment," I said, after showing him my Navy discharge papers.

He smiled at me. "Son, the Paras are just infantry who sometimes jump out of planes. It's physically tough but not exactly intellectually demanding." He smiled again. "You'd do better in something like the Royal Armoured Corps - still a combat function, but you need a bit more up top to be able to operate and maintain a main battle tank."

Mick was on temporary recruiting office duty. He was there to select recruits for all branches of the Army. But regimental loyalties are strong, even fierce, in the British Army, and he was just doing what recruiting sergeants have done for centuries—looking after the best interests of his own regiment. So I ended up enlisting in his regiment: the 3rd Royal Tank Regiment.

I was given a railway travel warrant at the recruiting office in Torquay and told to report to the Army's selection centre at Sutton Coldfield in early March, 1979. This was for two days of tests and interviews; the Army gave recruits a chance to choose alternative trades or regiments, depending on their success in the tests. My results were excellent and I could have picked from most of the skilled trades on offer. But I wanted to go into a combat regiment, and was posted on to the Royal Armoured Corps training depot at Catterick Garrison in Yorkshire.

The Royal Armoured Corps (RAC) is made up of the cavalry regiments and the Royal Tank Regiments (RTR) formed during the First World War. The RTR takes pride in having been the world's first tank regiment. They refer to the cavalry regiments (such as the 17/21st Lancers, and so on) as donkey wallopers, a derogatory reference to the horses they originally used. There were still a few units, such as the Household Cavalry, that still used horses for ceremonial duties. Otherwise, we were all equipped with the Chieftain main battle tank or Scorpion and Scimitar armoured reconnaissance vehicles.

I couldn't help thinking that winter wasn't the best time to begin basic military training on the Yorkshire moors. I tried to dismiss such thoughts as I watched the snow fall on the dreary landscape from the minibus taking me and the other recruits to Cambrai Barracks.

The barracks was named in honour of the battle of Cambrai, which took place on November 20, 1917). It was a relatively modern place, with decent accommodation with rooms shared between eight or nine recruits. The training staff came from the Royal Hussars, known as the cherry-pickers because they wore red trousers with their No2 uniforms.

There were also a few NCOs from the Army Air Corps, including Corporal Kayser, who was the drill instructor for our intake, which had the uninspiring title of 79/06. Our depot did the recruit training for the AAC, which was too small to have its own recruit training depot. Some of their lads thought they were going to end up being helicopter pilots one day. We pointed out that the nearest they would get to flying was washing the window in the front of a chopper, hence our nickname for them - bubble washers.

Having done recruit training with the Navy, I was well prepared for what was to come. There was a much bigger emphasis on physical fitness, especially cross-country running, assault courses, and the gym. Regardless of trade or specialisation, all soldiers were expected to have the basic skills and fitness to fight on foot. It was hard going at first, but I soon became accustomed to it.

The uniforms were different, but they still had to be washed, ironed, and folded, though not to the standards of HMS Ganges. If you could look after your kit there, all other military establishments are child's play by comparison. One thing that was new to me, though, was bulling boots.

Bulling boots was a skill that I acquired rapidly and then turned to my financial advantage. We were issued with the old-style ammunition boots, designed to be worn with puttees (long khaki fabric strips which were wound around the ankles at the top of the boot). Apart from the heels and toecap, the boots had a bubbled surface. The bubbles had to be flattened by covering the leather in polish and then burning it flat using the handle of a spoon that had been heated over a candle flame. The next stage was to cover the whole boot in a thick layer of black polish, which was briefly set alight to melt the surface till it was flat.

After the polish dried, it had to be bulled. We would wrap a damp yellow duster around the index finger and apply a little polish to the tip of the finger, and then gently rub in circles on the surface of the boot. Eventually, the surface of the boot took on a deep, burnished shine, like patent leather. A well-bulled pair of boots looked good placed at the end of your bed for kit and room inspections. Unfortunately, as soon as you wore them, the polish around the flexing part of the boots would crack and fall off.

Some lads couldn't get the hang of bulling, or couldn't be bothered. So, for twenty-five pounds, I would take someone's boots and bring them up to the standard required. It was a good little earner, and I managed to make enough from it for a holiday in Morocco.

Army parade drill differed from the Navy's. When marching, the Navy doesn't stamp the foot down; when coming to attention and so on, they just bring the heels smartly together. The timing is also different, but I picked it up without difficulty. The assault course caused me some problems initially, though. I'd done a few runs before joining, but when I hit the assault course, I realised I just wasn't fit enough. I wasn't the only one; some lads really struggled. But after lots of runs across the bleak Yorkshire moors I started to improve, and I found myself enjoying a new level of fitness and an enthusiasm for cross-country running.

We ran as a squad, along dirt tracks; through woodlands; across open, heather-covered fells; and through icy Yorkshire streams. It made me fitter but, just as importantly, it made me start to feel like an actual soldier.

Six weeks of basic training passed quickly. We then commenced trade training. Life became less restrictive, with less time spent on the parade ground. The AAC went off elsewhere for their training in advanced bubble washing or whatever it was they did, and the RAC soldiers joined the radio course.

Radio training was quite enjoyable. An easygoing sergeant instructor taught us voice procedures (VP) in the classroom. I'd used radios before in the Navy, so I was familiar with some VP, though, again, the Army had its own way of doing things. For instance, the Army way of checking effective communication between two radios was something like this:

"Hello, Three Four Charlie [34C], this is Whiskey Two Zero [W20] - radio check over."

34C would answer: "OK, over."

Then W20 would terminate with: "OK - out."

This was short and to the point. The Navy, by comparison, used archaic phrases like, "How d'ye hear me?" answered by, "Loud and clear, how me?"

We trained with Larkspur radio sets; some parts dated back as far as the late 1940s. One small flaw in the training was that the regiments were being re-equipped with modern Clansman sets, so when I joined my regiment, I didn't have a clue about the radios they used. But meanwhile I enjoyed a civilised four weeks in the classroom, a place relaxed enough to allow me time to read a paper at tea break. A civvy newsboy sold newspapers in the cookhouse during breakfast. Most lads bought the tabloids; I bought the *Daily Telegraph*. Because I had to have it specially ordered, I knew I was the only soldier in camp who did, though I think the officer's mess used to have one delivered. Every morning I marched across to training wing with my folded *Telegraph* under my left arm like a sergeant major's pace stick, to the amusement of *some* of the instructors.

After the radio course, we were divided for the next stage of trade training. Half our intake did a tank-driving course; the other half, which included me, did a gunnery course. It was predictably bullish. Every lesson started with us stood at attention. The instructor, Sergeant Wilkins, would shout, "It is the aim of this lesson to teach you, as gunner basics, the whatever whatever." We trained to maintain and fire the Chieftain's main armament, the 120mm gun, and the coaxially mounted 7.62mm general purpose machine gun. Some of the lessons were mundane, such as the cleaning and weapon-stripping tasks known to generations of soldiers. Some were some more interesting in a macabre way. One morning, Sergeant Wilkins got us together and held up a long rope.

"What's this?" he said.

"Track rope," someone answered quickly, wanting to keep him in a good mood.

"Well done, smartarse," Sergeant Wilkins said, looking pleased nonetheless. "But what else is it used for, apart from when you're changing a tank track?"

We answered the question with silence. So he told one soldier to climb inside the turret of the tank and showed us how to lift him out by threading the rope under his arms and in front of his chest. The object was to learn how to remove casualties from a tank hit by an anti-tank shell. As always, we had a good laugh doing things, though it was a little more sobering when he pointed out the real purpose.

"If a tank is hit and it brews up [burns], the crew are gonna be incinerated lumps of meat." He paused for emphasis. "An' believe me, you ain't gonna want to lift the bodies out by hand." But since we weren't expecting imminent combat, no one got too concerned about it.

The Chieftain tank was similar to its many predecessors. The gunner sat in the turret, on the right side of the gun's breech. The gun fired solid shot with a flat trajectory and a muzzle velocity of seventeen hundred metres per second, and a laser rangefinder determined the exact range from tank to target. In the hands of an experienced gunner, it was a deadly weapon system. Sadly, we rarely got to fire live ammunition, so expertise was hard to acquire.

At the end of the gunnery course, we went to the live firing range at Warcop in Cumbria. When my turn to act as loader came, I climbed into the turret. My mind turned into jelly, and everything I'd learnt went AWOL; I wished I could have followed it.

The gunner shouted, "Ranging sabot tank on!"

This indicated that he was firing the laser rangefinder. It was also the command for me to load an armour-penetrating, solid tungsten, tank-busting shell. My mind was blank, and my dismay must have been obvious. Sergeant Wilkins said slowly and calmly, "Don't flap, Widders."

My AWOL knowledge returned to duty, and I launched into a faultless set of loading drills. Now, if I ever feel myself in a panic, I bring Sergeant Wilkins' words to mind, and I'm back in control.

Later my turn came to sit in the gunner's seat. I enjoyed feeling the recoil of the whole sixty-ton tank as I fired at the redundant vehicles used as targets. Equally satisfying was the coaxial 7.62mm machine gun used against soft targets, like infantry. Of course, this was all very fine on the ranges, where no one was shooting back, but I was well aware that the real thing might be far less enjoyable.

When we got back to camp, we had to prepare for our final passing out parade. This entailed bulling already perfect boots and getting haircuts. I avoided my unnecessary trim by hiding in the NAAFI. Others were not so lucky.

On the big day, we paraded in No2 dress uniforms. We marched around the parade ground and were inspected by some visiting dignitary, whose name I can't recall now. The band played, the sun shone; adoring parents and girlfriends gazed on admiringly. Then we came to the part where we finally marched off the parade ground - this was where it all went to rat shit. The right hand marker, by whom we all kept pace and direction, thought we were too far ahead of the band. So he shortened the pace so drastically that we were virtually marching on the spot. Everyone ended up out of step, and we looked like a shower of shit, though not for the first time, according to our drill instructor.

We were all posted to our respective regiments, mine being the 3rd Royal Tank Regiment. I arrived in Paderborn along with another new trooper, Kev Harper. It was a bank holiday weekend, and no one wanted to know us, so we were left to our own devices for three days.

We had our training records with us in sealed envelopes, and I used my childhood skills to steam them open. My training report was excellent. I sealed it up and handed it in on Monday morning when I reported to my squadron.

I was part of C squadron, which was commanded by Major P. He put me straight on to a driver-training course that was already halfway through. Knowing that I'd been an NCO in the Navy, he wanted to get me fully trained up so that I could get promoted again. This was decent of him, and I appreciated it, though relations between us were to later go very sour indeed.

Starting in the middle of a course made things difficult. I spent a few days driving cross country, which was straightforward. Then we progressed to driving on roads. This was where the fun really started.

The driver of a Chieftain sits right in the front, looking out of a round hatch on the centreline of the tank. When driving cross country, this was fine, but I found it difficult to judge the tank's position on the road. Either I was too far to the right, bringing the tank close to the pavement, or too far left into the opposite lane.

"Mind that road sign," came the voice of the instructor over my headphones.

"What road sign?" I said, as sixty tons of tank flattened it.

"Now mind the pavement," he replied, and I noticed that the tracks were ripping chunks out of the kerb.

The following day, I saw a Volkswagen coming towards me. I was too far to the left, and there wasn't room for us both. I was less concerned than the driver of the car, who drove along the pavement. Can't blame him, really.

Soon after this, the regiment went out on exercise on a nearby training area. I was the gunner in call-sign 34Charlie - tanks were referred to by their radio call-sign - and I spent the weekend staring at the German countryside through a tank's gun sight. When we stopped to rest or for tactical reasons, we took turns on radio watch and on sentry duty. I should have found it all exciting and interesting, but I didn't.

At the end of the weekend Corporal Ray Conday walked up to me and said, "So, how did you enjoy your first exercise?" I could see in his eyes that he was surprised when I answered, "A bit boring, to be honest. It's not much fun sittin' in the gunner's seat for hours doing nothing."

I later heard a story about Ray. He was called to a tank commander's 'O' group--a briefing in the field. Needing to have a dump, he asked for permission to leave.

"You'll just have to wait," his troop leader replied.

"Can't, sir," answered Ray. He then dropped his coveralls and crapped, whilst the officer walked away speechless.

After the exercise, we returned to normal routine-maintenance and cleaning. Every morning, the squadron paraded by the tanks and was inspected by the OC. Then we'd break into individual troops (usually four troops of three tanks in a squadron), and work at maintaining our tanks. The drivers did automotive work and the gunners looked after the routine maintenance of the main armament. The radio operator did any work on the sets that might be required, and the commanders supervised. At midmorning, we would stop for tea break. At midday we would stop for dinner. Some of us would spend the dinner break in the NAAFI bar having a few beers before returning to work and finishing around 1630.

Each squadron had to provide men for guard duty. This meant being on guard about once every two weeks. No one liked it; it was just one of those jobs that had to be done. Guard was an overnight duty, starting after work. The new guard would parade by the guardroom by the main gate and be inspected by the orderly officer. The smartest man would be designated as stick man. He would be excused duties; this was an incentive to encourage a good turnout. The guy who almost inevitably got chosen was Melvyn Law, with his sewn-in creases and bulled boots. I usually came close, but there was no prize for second place.

Guard duty consisted of manning the gate (controlling access) or patrolling in pairs around the inside and perimeter of the camp. Patrolling was the better of the two duties to my mind. Standing by the gate in the early hours with nothing to do was tedious in the extreme. Patrolling was also an opportunity to plunder stores from other squadrons if they were foolish enough not to lock things away.

Guard duty finished the following morning at 0800, when the provost staff would take over. Then we went to shower and get breakfast before starting work at 0900.

It was whilst doing guard duty one day that I first met Captain Viccars. I noticed he had a stutter, which made his speech distinctive, especially on the radio. The lads told me a story about him and swore was true. It seems that Captain Viccars was orderly officer one day when a new trooper arrived to join the regiment.

"W-w-w what's your name?" Captain Viccars asked.

"M-m-m-m my n-n name is Trooper S.," replied the new trooper, who also had a stutter.

Each man's stuttering worsened. Captain Viccars assumed this guy was taking the piss and had him jailed, until someone caught on to it and sorted matters out. Viccars was generally popular with the lads. After I left the regiment, I heard that he became adjutant and had the squadron bars closed, which made his popularity plummet.

My troop leader was Lieutenant Regan. The troop sergeant was Paddy Kehoe, a good guy so long as you got the job done and didn't get on the wrong side of him. He came from the Republic of Ireland, which wasn't unusual in the British Army. Currently, around ten percent of the Army comes from other countries. The Gurkha regiments are recruited in Nepal. They're famous for their loyalty and courage on the battlefield, and have served with the British Army in both world wars and in more recent conflicts. The Gurkhas fight in their own regiments with British and Gurkha officers. But many British regiments have a smattering of soldiers from Commonwealth countries, such as South Africa, Fiji, and so on. My own regiment had a military band on attached duty, and they had a Zulu serving with them.

My regiment was meant to recruit from the West Country of England, from Cornwall through to Avon. This was a big area, which included some ethnically diverse areas like Bristol. So you might have expected 3RTR to have a bit of ethnic diversity, too.

Well you would be wrong; 3RTR was totally white. I don't know at what level it was decided, but there was a ban on recruiting blacks into the regiment. By contrast, the Royal Artillery Regiment in the barracks adjacent to us had large numbers of black soldiers. I suppose this was unjust, but at the time I didn't give a damn. So far as I know, neither did anyone else. I didn't know that it was a white regiment before I enlisted, but I seamlessly fell into and adopted the prevailing mores, totally failing to see any contradiction in my pride in being part of an elite, whites-only armoured regiment and my earlier disapproval of South African apartheid policies.

Regardless of colour, we were all discriminated against by the Germans. Paderborn was a nice, clean, prosperous middle-class town, with an ambivalent attitude towards hosting a British garrison. During the Second World War, our barracks had belonged to an SS Schutzstaffel, Nazi party combat troops. From 1945 onwards it was garrisoned by British troops, as were other barracks nearby. The British garrison brought a lot of money into the town and also employed quite a few Germans. The 'boxheads,' as we called them, seemed happy with that aspect of the garrison. But at the same time were not keen on the presence of large numbers of young soldiers. People spoke English in the shops and were happy to take our money. But some bars, restaurants, and all the discos displayed a sign at the door reading: "No Turks, No Greeks." Underneath this, it would state "out of bounds," a euphemism for "No British Soldiers." We didn't like this, but we grudgingly accepted it. Of course, we should have taken the bastards to court, alleging discrimination and claiming damages, but we were just young lads; we didn't know any better, and the people in charge of us didn't give a damn.

I'd gone to Germany intending to learn the language, so I enrolled in an evening class. But the squadron put me on guard duty during the second class. Most of the natives didn't want to speak with us anyway, so I gave it up. It's a shame, really. The few guys who persevered in learning the language had a much more rewarding time than the rest of us. Officially, the Army paid lip service to encouraging soldiers to learn the language, but I suspect the authorities were happier if we spent our off-duty time inside barracks, where we wouldn't cause any upsets with the locals.

Despite this, we used to go into town to various bars. But it was much cheaper to drink in the squadron bars or the NAAFI. The NAAFI (Navy, Army and Air Force Institutes) provided canteens and shop facilities for servicemen. We didn't always give them credit due for their hard work, and the acronym was also considered to stand for No Aptitude and Fuckall Interest!

The squadron bars were quite competitively priced, but the sergeant's mess practically gave its drink away - a bottle of local beer cost fifty pfennigs. This equalled eight bottles for a pound sterling, which was very cheap indeed. But one way or another, most of us relentlessly drank our wages away in camp - no doubt to the quiet satisfaction of both the locals and the Army.

Chapter Thirteen

Occasionally, civvies would comment that peacetime soldiering was safe and comfortable and a waste of their tax money. I would point out that soldiers pay tax, too, as their wages are no longer quite “starvation cheap,” as Kipling wrote in his poem “Tommy.” And even in so-called peacetime, soldiers get killed. Every year since the end of the Second World War, British soldiers have died in action somewhere.

But you don’t need a war to have casualties. I was the replacement for a man who died in my tank. I took over his job and was even issued with his blankets. The bedding storeman, another Liverpudlian called Lance Corporal F., thought he was a comedian. He put the blankets down on the counter, cracking, "Maybe you'll get killed like the lad who used to have them."

"Well if I do, you Scouse bastard," I replied, "I hope I get to take you with me."

Trooper French had helped bring my predecessor's body out of the turret in which he died, and Frenchy told me what had happened: My predecessor had leaned over the breech of the gun whilst the gun kit, or stabiliser, was switched on. The gun barrel depressed and the breech elevated, crushing his head between the massive steel breech and the armoured steel roof of the turret. He didn't live very long; according to Frenchy, his jaw moved up and down for a while as his body was lifted out via the commander's hatch. I didn't think much about the incident at the time. But I've wondered since how many civilians knew, or even cared, that my predecessor died in agony in my tank whilst guarding their freedom from the Soviet Army and communism.

Ironically, I very nearly crushed Frenchy under the gun in the exact same tank whilst out on exercise later in the year. There was a small access passage leading from the turret through to the driver's compartment in the front. The golden rule is never lean under, or over, the gun whilst the gun kit is switched on. If the gun kit throws a gremlin fit or the gunner decides to elevate the barrel, the breech comes down to the deck, and you can crush someone as easily under the breech as over it.

We were sat waiting for something or other - waiting was an art you become practised in as a soldier. Frenchy brewed up some tea and, unbeknownst to me, leaned under the breech to pass a cup through to the driver. I elevated the barrel of the gun and happened to glance to my left. "Fuckin' 'ell", I shouted to myself, as the breech came down onto Frenchy's neck. Frenchy gave a strangled squeak, which would have been his last one if I hadn't stopped and depressed the gun.

"You alright, mate?" I asked.

"Yeah, no problem," he said, taking his near demise with equanimity.

"Tell me the next time you're gonna lean under the fuckin' gun," I said, and we both laughed, though more with relief than humour.

But servicemen die all the time; helicopters fall out of the sky; vehicles driven by tired men crash. Accidental shootings, otherwise known as negligent discharges, don't happen often in the

British Army due to the high standards of weapon training. But the point I'm making is that even peacetime soldiering has its dangers. The West German conscript tank crews were renowned for having accidents. One German tank out on exercise drove over a hedge. The crew was unaware of the road on the other side and crashed down on top of a car, squashing its occupants.

There was supposedly a cut-off death rate during major exercises involving many thousands of troops and vast numbers of vehicles and aircraft. Rumour had it that a certain number of deaths were allowed for, and an exercise would only be cancelled if casualties went over that number. I can't hand-on-heart swear that this was true, but it's something we believed at the time.

The biggest exercise I was involved in was Exercise Red Gauntlet. Major manoeuvres were held to practice our response should our enemy, the Red Army, decide to move west. No one was under any illusions about our fate if this happened. The Warsaw Pact had a massive army of 775,000 active troops and two million reservists. We were stationed in West Germany to delay them long enough for large-scale reinforcements to be landed from the USA and Great Britain. We had technological superiority, but they had a vast numerical advantage. We felt confident we would achieve our objective and delay them, but our prospects of survival were minimal.

The regiment left barracks one wintry German morning as part of a much larger force; our enemy consisted of various other NATO units, playing the part of the Soviets. Leaving barracks in our sixty-ton Chieftain tanks was an interesting experience. It was the only time the locals seemed to look upon us in a decidedly friendly way. Our working dress was black coveralls, black boots, and black beret, attire that was similar to our SS predecessors in Barker Barracks, and I wondered if that accounted for the temporary change in attitudes.

An exercise like Red Gauntlet probably looked more exciting from the outside, to civilians, than it was to the soldiers involved. It had its moments, but for me, sat inside the turret, it was often profoundly boring. Since it was an exercise, I - obviously - couldn't fire at the enemy. So to judge the likely outcome of the various tactical manoeuvres, umpires raced around making judgments and deciding who was winning.

I'm sure this was all very exciting for the colonel and the squadron OC, etc. But to lowly old me, denied the opportunity to put my nominated enemy into the burning hell of a tank hit by an armour-penetrating round, time on the move was boring. So I resorted to my favourite recourse in times of tedium: reading. On this occasion, I read *Shardik* (something about a bear), plus an anthology of the works of D.H. Lawrence. This provided an ongoing source of amusement to the tank commander, Corporal Shelly Shelldrake. At quiet times, when he was bored, he would bring his moustachioed head back inside the turret and look over my shoulder. He would select a short passage from my book and mockingly relay it over the live intercom system. Mouse Hocking up front in the driver's seat would howl with laughter. I would abuse them for being a pair of idiot philistines, and then Mouse and I would have a beer.

We drank beer in prodigious quantities, which we bought on credit from the squadron quartermaster sergeant when he came around to issue rations. Mouse and I drank a lot even by squaddies' standards. At the end of Red Gauntlet, he had the highest beer bill in the squadron, followed by me. When the opportunity presented itself, we would go for something stronger than beer. It wasn't unusual at dawn stand-to for Mouse and me to drink vodka and grapefruit juice before moving off to rejoin the regiment from our lying up point. Mouse really shouldn't have been driving, but I couldn't envisage the German police stopping us to breathalyse him.

Halfway through the exercise, we had a change of tank commander. Corporal Bert Hammond replaced Shelly. He claimed to be the smallest man in the squadron, an honour disputed by me. Bert was more concerned about our alcohol consumption. He'd make plaintive comments, such as, "Don't you two overdo it, now," when one of us would shout "Snobby!"; this was the name of a small beer bottle, and the command for the radio operator to pass out a couple. There are only four men in a tank, and it's the commander's job to maintain discipline and control drinking, which was unofficially tolerated in moderation.

The radio operator was the fourth member of the crew, and his duties, in addition to operating the radio, were to provide in-flight catering. The key item in this was a box-like object called the boiling vessel, used to boil water to make brews and heat up tins of compo, the military rations we were issued with in the field.

The operator, Trooper 'Solly' Salisbury, would brew up tea on the move and make sandwiches. Our favourite type was ham-flavoured, processed tinned cheese, with tinned compo jam - usually with his trademark oily fingerprints on the bread.

We cooked more substantial meals on a petrol stove when we stopped at night and sometimes very early in the morning before moving off again. We did get some fresh food, but mostly we cooked tinned compo rations, carried in one of the storage bins on the side of the tank. The compo was issued in boxes, marked A, B, C, etc.; each one had a different main course, and our favourite was chicken curry. There were tinned vegetables and potatoes and so on, but to make life easier we often threw everything together into a stew.

It may well sound like a jolly camping and driving holiday, but it was hard work. A typical day would start before dawn, when we would receive orders by radio to move to our next position. On precious little sleep, we would take down the camouflage nets that we had slung from trees the evening before. We invariably boiled for a brew and sometimes cooked breakfast if there was time. We would have a token wash and a shave and pack away sleeping bags and any kit we had used. There might well be one of us stood sentry somewhere and someone else manning the radio. Four shell-scrapes had to be filled in; a shell-scrape is an individual trench long enough and wide enough for one man, and supposedly deep enough to offer some protection from blast and shrapnel. Then we would drive off.

Maybe we'd move, as part of a regimental formation, to another area. Maybe we would be part of an attacking force, going up against another armoured formation. Maybe we would go to lie up in a defensive position. Sometimes we would RV, or rendezvous, for a 'replen' - a meeting with elements of HQ squadron to replenish stores and top up with fuel. Mouse would be driving for long hours most days, and the commander would be listening to two radio networks and map reading and so on. I'd be staring through the bloody gun sight all day looking for the enemy. None of these things are especially arduous in themselves. But add in a few days sleep deficit and the subzero temperatures of a German winter and it becomes less of a jolly camping trip and more like hard work.

At night, we would usually go into a wooded area, where it would be easier to camouflage tanks and stay hidden. This might be as part of our troop of four tanks or part of a squadron or regimental formation. Sometimes we would knock down small trees with the tank and use them as camouflage. We also used camouflage nets, strung between trees and propped up with long poles. Usually, two of us would set up the cam nets whilst the other two dug shell scrapes, prepared a meal, or made a shelter for sleeping. There might be other tasks, such as engine maintenance or tightening the tank tracks and so on - we kept busy. By the time all this was done it would usually be dark, though sometimes it might be night-time before we even started. Sometimes we had to keep going through the night. It all depended on the tactical situation.

We often slept on the back decks of the tank. Steel-armoured ventilation grills covered the engine and generator. They retained the engine heat for hours and made a warm but uncomfortable place to kip. Sometimes we just slept out on the ground. Different crews had different preferences - it was up to us to make ourselves comfortable.

Once ensconced inside my slug (sleeping bag), I was reluctant to quit it for anything minor like a bit of rain. The easiest thing was to wriggle around, put the waterproof base of the bag on top, and just sleep through it.

But we would never get unbroken sleep. There was sentry duty or radio watch during the night, usually for a couple of hours at least, depending on the number of tank crews sharing the duties. We might well receive orders to move during the night or have to stand to in the face of an attack.

When under attack from infantry, the best advice is to start the tank's engine. No grunt likes the idea of running around in the woods at night with tanks moving near him, so they tended to get out of the way in case we actually did move. When dawn came, we would pack up, take down the nets, and so on, and the whole cycle would start again.

We had a few automotive problems during Red Gauntlet. This wasn't unusual with the Chieftain tank. Within the first few days, we changed the main engine and then the generator. This was done with the aid of the Royal Electrical and Mechanical Engineers Light Aid Detachment (REME LAD). The REME fitters lifted out the engine, using the crane fitted on their FV432 series recovery vehicle. The engine was designed to be lifted out and changed under battle conditions, so it was a relatively straightforward process. Meanwhile, I was happy with a change in routine and the chance to be out of the turret.

Later in the exercise, disaster struck as our troop was on the move. Of course, it depends on your perspective - to me, disaster was an opportunity. But to Lieutenant Regan, who got us into the mess, it wasn't such good news. We were driving along a dirt track, bordered on either side by a deep ditch with a stream. We'd been warned that it wasn't strong enough to take the weight of tanks, but the troop leader was in a hurry to get to the RV. So he decided to take a chance.

The first two tanks advanced at a steady speed down the track. We followed a couple of hundred yards behind, with Mouse doing his best to keep us away from the ditches. Then the tank started to tilt to the right as the track collapsed into the deep ditch. I watched the horizon shift to a crazy angle through the gun sight. "Jesus fuckin' Christ," I muttered to myself, "looks like we're tippin' over." Sixty tons of Chieftain tank was never designed to do this, and I rapidly pondered my chances of survival. Would the turret detach itself? Would I be stuck inside with the hatches blocked? Would the fuel from an upside-down engine leak and ignite? I debated the wisdom of climbing up from the gunner's seat and scrambling past the commander to get out of the hatch. Then the movement stopped. Our tank settled back down again, resting at an angle in the collapsed ditch.

Wisely, the tank behind us reversed and got out of the ditch. Lieutenant Regan, in the lead tank, stopped further up the track. The radio buzzed with reports and explanations, whilst I sat there and enjoyed the odd-angle view of Germany through my gun sight. Then I climbed out, still clutching my anthology of the works of D.H. Lawrence, whilst Mouse again tried to drive out of the ditch.

Our tank never budged an inch. The front jammed into the mud, and the left track spun in the air. So we did what generations of soldiers have done in situations like this - we brewed up and had tea. Then a major from the Royal Engineers appeared to assess the situation. He walked up and saw the book held in my left hand.

"No wonder your bloody tank gets in a mess if the crew spend their time reading that filth," he said. We both laughed, and then he headed off to confer with his own guys.

A Chieftain armoured recovery vehicle appeared a few hours later. The ARVE is a Chieftain tank chassis with a big winch instead of a turret, designed to recover damaged tanks from the battlefield. It was crewed by our own REME fitters. They thought our predicament the funniest thing they'd seen for a long time. So did we.

We stretched steel-wire towing hawsers from the two towing hooks on the front of our tank to similar tow points on the rear of the ARVE. With this done, I stood with the growing crowd of military and civilian onlookers, watching as the ARVE edge forward, taking up the strain on the tow. Mouse was back in the driving seat of our tank. He went into first forward gear to assist, and we all cheered as our tank went nowhere and the ARVE sunk into the dirt track on its left side.

So now we had a ruined road, and over one hundred tons of stranded vehicles. It was getting dark, and we were clearly going nowhere. No doubt someone, somewhere, was deeply concerned about all this. But to the crews, it was a welcome break in routine. For us, the war was over. So we set a sentry to guard the vehicles, went down to the nearby village, and bought some beers.

Actually, some of us bought quite a lot of beer. One of the REME fitters fell asleep and couldn't be roused. We dragged him by the heels into some kind of private meeting room where the local equivalent of the women's institute was sat in a large semicircle. We left him lying on the floor, arms folded, Sterling submachine gun on his chest, surrounded by thirty middle-aged German *hausfraus.*

The next day, another ARVE got bogged in trying to get us out. But all good things come to an end, and eventually we dug all the vehicles out and rejoined the exercise. Before we left, I got a copy of the local newspaper and proudly took away the photo of my tank. Being that it was written in German, I didn't understand most of the accompanying article. But the headline was clear: "400,000 Deutschmarks worth of damage in the Bornhausen area."

We rejoined the manoeuvres. Solly was replaced by Lance Corporal Garret-West, otherwise known as G-Dubs. Soon after this, Bert started the rebmit joke, shouting timber backwards, which earned our crew a bollocking for not taking the exercise seriously. When tanks stop for any length of time, they need to be camouflaged, as static vehicles are vulnerable to attack from aircraft and artillery. Even on the move, tank crews sometimes hang vegetation off the sides and throw turf over the glacis plate (the sloping armour in front of the tank). They use camouflage nets when stationary. But it's not always easy to hide something that big. The ideal place is a wood, with lots of thick vegetation and overhead cover.

Forests come in all shapes and sizes. On a good day, some appear to have been planted by the God of soldiers. The trees are spaced far enough apart to drive between, with branches at just the right height to hang camouflage nets from. You then try to hide the tank tracks that lead into the woods. You dig shell scrapes, set a radio watch, and sit there praying that the God of soldiers will continue to bless you, and that you will be forgotten and sit out the rest of the exercise doing bugger all.

But there often isn't enough space between the trees to get through, so you just knock them over with your tank. Then, when your tank is in place, you try to hide the damage to prevent giving away your position. The four of us would struggle to erect a tree, howling with laughter and shouting "Rebmit!" like lumberjacks working in reverse. Just then the RSM appeared, and it was a bollocking all round. It probably sounds daft, but in the middle of a miserable German winter, when you feel cold, wet, and tired, the little things keep you going.

Chapter Fourteen

Germany was getting boring. So I decided to desert and go to Africa to find work as a mercenary. My co-conspirator in this stupid plan was Mouse Hocking. He didn't have a passport, so he sent off a passport application to England, enlisting the help of his mother, who was unaware of his reason for wanting one.

Meanwhile, Mouse continued with regimental duties; I went on Operation Snow Queen in Bavaria. Basically this was skiing, dressed up as military training. It consisted of four weeks of downhill and cross-country ski training. After a couple of weeks, I got quite good, especially at the langlauf (cross country) and was able to help instruct beginners.

One day I took one of our officers on a cross country ski trail. He was doing everything correctly, as I'd shown him, but he just couldn't keep up. "Come on, sir, put some fuckin' effort into it!" I kept shouting back at him. To his credit, he was giving it one hundred percent. His arms and legs were going like pistons, and sweat was pouring off him. Then the reason suddenly occurred to me. I turned back and waited for him. "'Ang on sir, let me check yer skis," I said.

"What's the joke, Widders?" he said, as I fell about laughing. Then I explained that wax should be applied to the base of the skis to give traction in the snow; his skis were smooth and wax-free.

Mouse came out for a couple of week's ski training too. We confided our little plan to do a runner to one of the cooks. He thought this was a great laugh and gave us a small suitcase full of compo rations to take with us. This included tinned tropical butter, which didn't melt even when we crossed the Sahara desert, though I shudder now to imagine what must have been added to it.

When we returned to Paderborn, Mouse's passport had arrived, sent from his unsuspecting mother. I knew that our kit lockers would be searched when our absence was discovered, so I put some of my personal possessions in a bag and left it with Ted Wolfe, a married trooper who lived in quarters with his wife. It was decent of him to look after my stuff, as he would have got into a stack of trouble if found out.

We needed to buy train tickets, so we took a trip downtown to the Bahnhof. We wanted to be out of Germany by the time our absence was discovered; hitching was likely to be problematic and slow, so Bundesbahn it was.

I looked up the German for “ticket” in my little phrase book and presented myself at the ticket window. “Swei karte aus Algeciras bitte,” I said.

The ticket man looked a bit surprised. He looked through his book and discovered that Algeciras was in southern Spain, and then sold us tickets for the following evening. We couldn’t go downtown without having a few beers, so we went into a bar and planned the best way to get out of camp the next day. Then it was back to barracks to pack our kit and get some kip.

The following morning, we paraded with the rest of the squadron and went about our daily work on the tank park. Time dragged, and I think we both felt a little nervous. A couple of the lads knew what we were up to, but no one in authority did or we'd certainly have been stopped by then. Eventually 1600 came, and we went back to the block to shower and collect our kit. We'd decided to travel light, carrying only sleeping bags and a few spare clothes. I took a couple of books, including one on Tibetan meditation, and Mouse took a few hundred fags.

Walking through the barrack gate carrying bergans (backpacks) would invite questions, so we put them inside bin bags and went out the back gate. Mouse turned to one of the sentries. "We're taking laundry out to be washed at a place in town," he said, holding up his black bin bag. Once outside, we jumped a taxi down to the Bahnhof and got a much-needed beer, plus a carry-out for the train ride.

We were both relieved when the train left the station. I can't remember what we talked about - it was probably beer-fuelled nonsense and bravado. The next morning, we arrived in Paris and briefly discussed applying to join the French Foreign Legion. Having made some enquiries, I knew that the recruiting centre was in Vincennes and you could present yourself to any gendarmerie and be sent on. Some long-overdue common sense crept in at this point, and we dismissed the idea and took the metro to another station to get our connection to Spain.

We arrived at the French-Spanish border early in the evening and crossed on foot through the Spanish customs post into Irun. The customs officer looked at our bag of tinned Army compo rations with deep and undisguised suspicion. He rattled a tin with "sweets and chocolate" written on the lid. Clearly sceptical, he told us to open it, which we did, using a little Army issue compo can opener. I proffered one of the bars of fruit and nut chocolate, which he declined. He grudgingly waved us through, and we went into town to look for a bar.

We found a quiet bar and sat down with a couple of beers. I asked the barman to put on some Pink Floyd. During a pause between tracks on the album, a Spanish guy came in and sat on a barstool. The silence was suddenly broken by the cacophony of alarm clocks that begins "Money," and the surprised Spaniard fell off his stool. Some beers and a good laugh at Johnny Foreigner was just what we needed. Then we went to the station and took the train to Milan.

We arrived the following morning in blazing sunshine and enjoyed a stroll, followed by some junk food and wine for breakfast. Our next train left later in the day and finally deposited us, grimy and tired, in Algeciras.

Getting a ferry to North Africa was easy enough; the waterfront was crowded with little travel agencies. We bought a couple of tickets and got straight onto a ship to Morocco. I'd been to Tangiers before, so when we landed, the hassles weren't a shock to me. But the stream of touts that followed us to the seafront hotel irritated Mouse. I remembered them well from my last trip.

After checking in, we took a stroll, and an Arab tout who wanted to sell us some hashish followed us. We allowed the Arab to lead us to some dodgy cafe in the Kasbah to do business and have a mint tea.

"Barbara Hutton visited here many times," he said, giving us the tourist crap about the Woolworth heiress.

"Never heard of the bitch," replied Mouse. "Now let's have a smoke." The Arab rolled a joint, Mouse and I tried it, and Mouse signalled his approval.

We bought some of the hash the Arab used to make the joint. Or at least we thought we had. When we tried it later, we realised that he'd switched it with something else, despite us watching him very carefully. The rubbish he'd given us wasn't dope - the only dopes were us. I've never smoked camel dung, but that's what we speculated our dealer friend sold us.

We tried hitching when we left Tangiers. It wasn't hard to get people to stop, but they wanted money. Many of the local people travelled like this, but we were trying to travel on the cheap and didn't want to pay. It just didn't work, so eventually we gave up and took various buses east into Algeria. Much of the detail now escapes me. We stayed at various towns and villages, including Sidi Bel Abbess, the former home of the French Foreign Legion in colonial

North Africa. At this stage we were enjoying travelling, in the same sense that a genuine tourist might. We didn't have any doubts or concerns- - yet.

Hitching lifts was easier in Algeria, a more affluent place than dirt-poor Morocco. Since it was a socialist country with travel restrictions, people seemed keen to meet foreigners, and no one tried to rip us off or hassle us.

Other travellers shared parts of our journey south as we headed down the main trade route through the central Sahara. We met an Englishman who was crossing the Sahara on foot, and another man on a budget so low that he was virtually begging his way around the world. He teamed up with us for a couple of days, and we watched with amazement as he cajoled free meals for us all in roadside cafes and stalls. I suppose at heart, though, we were still soldiers, despite our absence from the regiment, so we parted company - begging was something we didn't take to easily. Soldiers are trained to be self-reliant, and we also had plenty of self-respect. So we preferred to pay our own way, despite the fact that our money was running out far more rapidly than we had expected. At times, too, I questioned the wisdom of what we were doing. Deep down, I knew that it had been wrong to leave the regiment, but I put the thought to the back of my mind.

In the more populated northern region of the Atlas Mountains, we stayed in hamams. They were steam baths during the day; then, at night, mattresses were laid out for sleeping. It was great to have hot water to luxuriate in after a long, hot, dusty day. Hamams were also clean and comfortable, unlike one hotel we slept in whose sheets displayed the evidence of months of previous occupants, prompting us to sleep on the floor. Further south in the desert, we'd get lifts in cars or trucks and stay at oasis towns like Ghardaia and El Golea. At night we walked into the desert, rolled out sleeping bags, and slept under the stars.

One morning, Mouse played a good joke on me. It was my habit in the morning to wander off behind a rock or sand dune to have a crap. With a brilliant piece of silent stalking, he crept around behind me and photographed me squatting in the desert. It was the sort of daftness that amused us then, and the photo later got a good laugh in the squadron bar.

Eventually, we arrived at a one camel oasis called In-Salah. We sold a bottle of whisky (at a fat profit) to the locals, who couldn't readily get access to alcohol. Nonetheless, our funds were getting low. So we sat down and thought through our situation. We had enough money to get to West Africa and maybe further on to the Congo. We hadn't a clue about how, or where, to find work as mercenary soldiers. The most likely prospect was ending up destitute somewhere and having to surrender ourselves to a British Consulate. We guessed what would have followed: at best, being held under open arrest - and at worst, being locked up in some African hellhole jail at the behest of some bloody diplomat, whilst a four-man escort was flown from Germany to bring us back. We'd been away for nearly three weeks, and the reality of our situation was beginning to hit home. So we made our first sensible decision: we agreed to return to the regiment.

Decision made, we walked up to the narrow, potholed bit of tarmac and hitched a lift north on one of the trucks coming up from the Nigerian border. We eventually crossed into Tunisia, and spent a day in Tunis, visiting the ruins of Carthage, taking turns photographing each other standing behind a headless statue in the amphitheatre. Then, our nod to culture satisfied, we took ferries to Sicily and then to the Italian mainland.

Hitchhiking in Italy proved difficult; no one would stop. We had a pizza in a little cafe and then tried to sleep the night in the waiting room of a railway station. A couple of hours later, two Italian railway officials swinging heavy metal chains made it clear that we weren't welcome. This was a shame, as I had traveller's diarrhoea and wasn't feeling too good. But the wisest thing was bugger off and come back in the morning.

The next day, we spent the last of our money on tickets to Munich. The train changed at Bologna. We walked around, gazing longingly at the fantastic cake shops in the arcades. With our compo rations long gone and all our money spent, it was a hungry journey onwards as we got the connection to Munich.

The train pulled into Munich Hautbahnhof in the early evening. We strolled around and then went back to the station waiting room. It was full of drunks and drug addicts, who were also planning to shelter there for the night. Sat amongst them was a worried-looking Briton. All of the hotels were booked solid for the Beer Festival, and he was stuck in the station with a courier bag full of company documents. He asked us to keep an eye on him for the night. In return, he took us to a nearby *bier haus* for a couple of drinks and some much appreciated food.

Later, back at the station, our new pal slept on the waiting room floor wrapped around his bag, and we sat on either side of him until the German *politzei* came in at 0600. They shouted "Raus Raus*!*" ("Out! Out!") like ham actors in an old POW war film. But we knew the German police were not to be messed with, and we left with everyone else. We said goodbye to our new mate, knowing he'd be safe enough now, and left the station.

We walked from the station and found a road that headed north. There was a branch of the Sparkasse bank nearby. We walked in and asked for the balance of our accounts. It was worth a try, but, predictably, they were both empty. To my surprise, the bank clerk offered us an advance of ten Deutschmarks each, which we converted to bratwurst and chips at a nearby *schnellimbiss,* or fast food street stall.

We got our first lift in a truck. At midday, we ended up at a motorway service station, standing at the exit with thumbs out. A police car pulled up and one of the policemen asked what we were doing. I explained that we were making our way back from Africa to our regiment in Paderborn. Naturally, I omitted the fact that we were AWOL. Our Army ID cards were inspected and returned, and the police left, cheerfully ignoring the fact that we were breaking the law by hitching on an autobahn.

Mouse suggested that we split up to make getting a lift easier, and we arranged to meet back in camp. I soon got a lift and eventually ended up on the outskirts of Paderborn. A few minutes later Mouse appeared, having been dropped off just down the road.

"What now?" I asked Mouse. Neither of us felt too worried. We knew we were going to end up in jail; the only question was exactly when. We decided to get into camp by scaling the wall at a quiet spot where some trees would give us cover. What we didn't know was that the IRA had recently shot and killed a soldier in Germany, and all garrisons were on heightened alert, with extra-armed sentries. We waited till dusk, watching the road alongside the camp. Then we ran to the wall and climbed over and darted into the cover of some trees. A few minutes later, we casually emerged onto the road and walked openly past RHQ, heading towards the barrack accommodation blocks. I felt a bit tense, and it took a good deal of self-control to stroll casually. But we needed to avoid drawing attention to ourselves--and we also wanted to avoid being shot by our own sentries.

Everywhere seemed very quiet. Then the penny dropped: we realized the regiment was out on exercise, meaning the camp wasn't empty. There are always some troops left doing security duties, and there are HQ detachments doing pay and so on. But it was quiet enough for us to get to our rooms without being seen.

Locking the door again, we sat on our beds and together breathed a sigh of relief. I took a look at my kit locker, which had been opened. My kit was mostly still there, though someone had plundered a few bits and pieces, including my leather Northern

Ireland gloves. We searched the room and collected up some small change, which totalled up to a couple of Deutschmarks—enough to buy a couple of cheese rolls from the NAAFI vending machines. Going to the NAAFI would be taking a risk, but when you're hungry, you do what it takes. We hadn't had much food in the last couple of days, and my stomach was beginning to wonder if my throat had been cut!

Later in the evening, we walked over to the NAAFI and spent our pfennigs. We didn't bump into anyone, but as we returned to the blocks, we heard footsteps. We hid in a recess and looked out to see Kev Harper, who had been excused going on exercise for some reason. He was shocked to see us and reluctantly agreed to help out by getting us some food.

In the morning, we had the bright idea of sending someone down to the Sparkasse Bank office in the RHQ building to see if we had been paid again. Kev had told one or two others about our return, and someone volunteered to enquire at the bank for us. He said the bank clerk reckoned that we'd been paid and our accounts were in credit. It seemed too good to be true. But, nonetheless, we came up with another of our little plans. It was too risky going to the bank in RHQ ourselves, so we decided to break out of camp the following day, go to the main bank to withdraw the cash, and then go off somewhere again. That was just a daft impulse. If the money had been there we'd have gone off to spend our cash, and then come back to face the inevitable.

The next day, we openly walked towards the back gate out of camp. A challenge came from an armed patrol. They were from a different squadron, which was lucky, as they didn't recognise us. We showed our ID cards and concocted some story about going out to visit some girls whose husbands were away in the married quarters. This amused them, and they left us to it. We strolled casually out the gate.

At the bank, we showed ID and demanded whatever money was in our accounts. The clerk checked in some sort of ledger. When he came to my name, he looked surprised and said, "Wait." Then he rushed into a back room. Obviously the game was up, so we got out sharpish. Unknown to us, some bloody administrative clerk from RHQ was passing by at the same time. We later discovered that he recognised us and went back to report his sighting. But we didn't know this then, so there seemed little else to do but wait until dark and make a covert entry back into camp.

Later in the evening, we were sat in one of the empty rooms watching the television; coincidentally, the programme was called *Enemy at the Door.* Then a knock came on our door. There wasn't time to think about things or be worried. We opened the door to find Sergeant Lindores, the duty sergeant, and some of the guard. Sgt. Lindores looked a little nervous - he must have wondered if we were going to resist arrest. The lads on guard-duty were impassive, though I knew they'd be gagging to find out where we'd been. We were arrested, a more informal and common occurrence than in civvy street, and taken to the guardroom. Later on, we were taken back to collect our mattresses and wash kit before being locked up for the night.

The cells were little changed from when the building had been the SS Panzer Regiment's guardroom during World War II. A bare room with a wooden sleeping platform was about all there was in each cell. The corner cell had a high barred window; we were to spend the next month there, and it became my favourite cell, as it was possible to look outside and felt less claustrophobic than the others.

The following day, Mouse and I were brought up in front of the orderly officer, though we both declined to say anything. We knew that seeing the colonel was inevitable. He commands the regiment, and he has the power to award the biggest punishments. But the colonel was away, so we were held under close arrest until his return.

Being in cells under close arrest isn't much fun, locked up alone all night and then taken out during the day to work. But we were legally innocent until proven guilty, and now that we were back with the regiment awaiting trial, we began receiving pay again - ot that we would actually get our hands on any money for some time to come. We never discovered why the bank had said that our accounts were in credit earlier; they certainly weren't.

All regiments have their own cells. Some are much, much worse than others, and some infantry regiments have a reputation for being very harsh. We used to see the prisoners from the Royal Artillery Battery carrying large packs and being beasted all over their side of camp. Our jail was pleasant by comparison. The unwritten rule was: behave yourself, don't cause problems, and no one will make life any more difficult than it has to be.

In the mornings, we neatly folded our kit (which was minimal) and laid it on the floor for inspection. Then we would be marched to the cookhouse by the provost staff, for breakfast, and marched back out again. After this, we would be given some sort of work to be done under supervision.

When our close arrest commenced, we were asked if we were willing to work. Army regulations stated that soldiers under close arrest and unable to carry out normal squadron duties couldn't be forced to carry out other work unless they agreed to it. But refusal would have resulted in hours spent being beasted in the gymnasium by some bloody PTI, and then being marched and drilled around camp for the rest of the day by the provost sergeant or corporal.

We wisely elected to work, and often this wasn't too bad at all. Sometimes we washed dishes in the cookhouse under the supervision of Norman, the cook sergeant from the Catering Corps. He was a bit effeminate in his mannerisms, and I often wondered if he was gay. These mannerisms weren't enough to bring him into conflict with the authorities: If he'd been part of the regiment, instead of being attached personnel, it would have been a very different story.

Years later, I bumped into him at an ATM in Wendover, Buckinghamshire. "Hello, Norman," I said cheerily: "Still in the Army?"

"No--they didn't want me anymore," he replied. He was reticent about the details, but his obvious bitterness when he told me he'd been forced to leave the Army spoke volumes.

Homosexuality certainly wasn't prevalent in the Army, where it was an offence against military law. Also, anyone known to be gay would have been at serious risk of being beaten up in most regiments. The law is different now, though. Parliamentary equal opportunity legislation means that it is no longer a military offence, though anyone openly gay is probably likely to suffer unpleasant consequences from other soldiers.

The only other case I heard about was with the RTR band, which was based in our barracks. One day I heard that four of them were in jail due to some carry-on between them. But they were musicians, on attachment to the regiment. Personnel on attachment, like cooks and bandsmen, fulfilled a role working for the regiment, but weren't truly part of it. They didn't really have to fit in with the accepted regimental values, and differences and eccentricities were more likely to be overlooked.

We often worked in the sergeant's and warrant officer's mess. Beastie Sutherland, the mess corporal, used to come to the guardroom, sign for us, and then march us up to the sergeant's mess to do whatever jobs there were. Beastie was really easygoing. He'd often buy us a bottle of Paderborner Pilsner at lunchtime, which we drank while hiding in the cellar.

At around 1600, we'd be returned to the guardroom. During the day, it was manned by the regimental provost staff, who functioned like police. The provost corporal was a bit authoritarian and we tried to avoid him. The provost sergeant was Rick Pickering. As his name suggested, he came from Yorkshire and spoke with a pronounced accent. Rick would leave the cell doors open during the early evening and at weekends. We'd mingle with the lads on guard duty and do odd jobs like sweeping up or making coffee.

Sometimes a shout would come from the guardroom: "Hocking, Widders - two coffees, one black, no sugar, and one NATO." NATO meant milk and two sugars. Rick was a nice guy who treated us well and elected not to notice when we mimicked his accent, asking him to repeat what kind of coffee he wanted.

Our own regimental staff ran the jail, and normally only 3RTR soldiers were locked up in it. However, one day, a couple of gunners from the Royal Artillery camp next door were sent in. Later that evening, we had a chance to sit together and have a cup of tea before being locked up for the night.

A tall skinny gunner, with highly polished boots, sat down next to me. "Why are you here pal?" I asked.

"Our jail is full," he said, "which is good news, as your jail is much easier than ours."

I knew this was true, as I'd seen their prisoners being really beasted, running around camp in full webbing and carrying rifles above their heads.

"What did you do to get jailed?" I said.

He told me - and I was really impressed. He'd gone downtown (at night) to the *Rathaus,* or town hall, where there was a temporary exhibition of paintings by Salvador Dali. He'd climbed onto the roof, broken in through a skylight, and stolen one of the paintings. Then he called the civvy police from a phone box, telling them where it was, which was how he got caught.

"But why did you do it?" I asked.

"Drunk and bored, mate," he said with a laugh.

I asked the other gunner what he'd done - and he was even crazier than his oppo. He'd taken a tracked armoured personnel carrier, driven it to the centre of town, and then driven over and crushed a row of parked cars.

Soon after this, C squadron returned from exercises. We were marched in front of the OC, Major P. To say that he was intensely pissed off with us would be to put it mildly. He raged at us, saying (rightly) that we'd failed in our duty and let down our comrades and so on. We both formally declined to state our case, as was our right. Any defence was pointless; it was inevitable that we would go in front of the colonel.

Major P took it all very, very, personally. Long after, when I was in another squadron, he wouldn't even allow me to enter the C squadron accommodation block to visit a friend. He also used his rank to cause problems for me. This certainly wasn't the norm in the Army. Usually, once the official punishment was complete, you were given the chance to settle down and do your job. Many years later in civvy street, I worked as a teacher alongside Toby Adamson, a former officer from B squadron. He suggested that Mouse and I might have had an adverse effect on P's career - he certainly never made colonel. When I think of that, I can understand his anger.

Four weeks after we were put under close arrest, the colonel returned from wherever. We were sent for and left standing at ease outside his office in RHQ. The regimental colours stood in a glass case nearby, saluted by anyone passing, a silent reminder of our ignominy. I can't remember if we were marched in separately or together. The colonel peered at me over the top of his half-moon spectacles. He asked if I was guilty.

"Yes, sir," I said.

"Do you have anything to say for yourself?"

"No, sir," I answered, staring at a spot on the wall behind him, wishing he'd get on with it.

The colonel stared at me. "You are a gypsy, Widders. You'll never settle down to anything and you'll never come to any good." He gave me a final glare over the top of those bloody glasses, and said, "Awarded twenty-eight days in the Military Corrective Training Centre. March him out, RSM."

Mouse received different comments but the same sentence, and we were both marched back to cells. I didn't give the colonel's comments much thought at the time, but he had a point about my wandering "gypsy" nature: nearly three decades later, I'm still on the move from place to place.

We'd known that we would end up in the glasshouse. The only surprise was the sentence; we'd expected longer. Army regulations stated that our sentences commenced immediately, regardless of where we were. So no time was lost getting transport, and two days later we found ourselves on a flight to England. A couple of lads from another squadron were detailed to act as escort on the journey.

Rick Pickering gave us a friendly farewell admonition in his broad Yorkshire accent. "Now, don't misbehave on the way, will you?"

"Don't worry, Rick, we'll be good boys," we joked, and got into the back of the transit van taking us to the airport.

On arrival in England, we were handed over to an escort from MCTC. They put us in the back of an Army four-ton Bedford lorry, along with a few others also en route to a holiday in the glasshouse. Arriving was less of a shock than I'd imagined. There was little screaming and shouting and being beasted about - just a quick medical inspection and a bedding issue. We soon discovered the old unwritten rule applied here, too; do as you're told, don't buck the system, and life will not be made more unpleasant than it need be. That said, even at its best, twenty-eight days in a military prison is not what I'd recommend to anyone wanting a good time.

The day consisted of three main activities: parade drill, physical training, and education. In the evening and lunch break, we cleaned kit and bulled boots. Most days commenced with an hour or so in the classroom, followed by lots of square bashing. There were a handful of RAF lads amongst us, the RAF not being blessed with its own prison, and their attempts on the parade square often had even the hard-faced drill instructors laughing. Physical training (PT) consisted mostly of cross-country runs, which I enjoyed. To my surprise, they were done in open countryside, outside the prison perimeter.

On the first run, our instructor advised us: "If you decide to run away, it isn't too difficult, and I won't even try to stop you." (I didn't believe that bit.) "But when you are eventually caught and brought back, you will truly wish you'd never been born."

The last bit I did believe, and I never contemplated scarpering during the cross-country runs, and no one else ever did - at least whilst Mouse and I were there.

The prisoners lived in rows of huts, with bars on the windows and doors that locked from the outside. Each hut held about ten men. There was a row of beds on each side of the room and a big, black coal-burning stove in the middle. A barbed wire fence surrounded the camp, emphasising the feeling of imprisonment with bleak finality.

MCTC had been built to hold German and Italian prisoners of war during World War II. I really wouldn't have been too surprised to see Steve McQueen pop up from a tunnel beneath the potbellied stove in the room. The stove burned coal, and, not surprisingly, it got dirty. At least it would have, had we ever lit it. Since it had to be cleaned every morning and burnished to a high gloss using shoe polish, we agreed to cut down on work, of which there was no shortage, by putting up with the cold at night.

Each soldier was issued with two sheets, three blankets, and two pillows. Every morning they had to be folded one on top of another, with razor sharp creases, making a square-shaped bed block which we placed at the top of the mattress. It took time and effort to fold the blankets, and, as time was limited and the consequences of getting it wrong were not good, most of us didn't use the blankets for sleeping at all. We left them folded underneath the bed and slept using the sheets and the bedside mat we each had been issued. It wasn't much of a piece of carpet - just enough to cover the top half of the body. So I lay in bed the first night, clutching a piece of carpet over me. *Oh, well, better than soddin' nothing*, I thought, mentally cursing both the Army and my own stupidity for getting myself into this mess. Then tiredness took over and I slept.

Uniforms were kept folded up in a wooden box at the end of the bed. Every morning, the prison staff inspected the whole lot: room, stove, beds, boxes, and so on.

We were allowed to send a certain number of items of kit to a laundry. Every Saturday, the dirty laundry was collected and the clean returned. Most of us would simply send the laundered items, still wrapped and untouched, straight back again. The object was to reduce the amount of kit held in the locker. The less you had, the less work folding, ironing, and keeping it neat in a small wooden box.

Mail was censored and making specific references to life in MCTC itself was forbidden. When my family wrote to me, the prison staff opened the letters before handing them to me in the cookhouse at meal times.

The prisoners were divided into different wings. If you were there long enough (we weren't), you would be moved on to another wing with a less restrictive routine, subject to good behaviour. Soldiers with long sentences were put on training courses, such as the small arms instructors' course, the ethos being rehabilitative, not just punitive. Most of the soldiers were there for the same reason as Mouse and me, going AWOL, so it wasn't like a civilian prison, full of criminals. Life wasn't great, but it could have been much worse; the time passed quickly enough.

Good behaviour earned remission - two days, in our case. We were brought in front of the CO for a discharge interview. He said that we were going back to the regiment with a clean slate and that we should work hard and so on and so on. We were discharged and sent to the Royal Armoured Corps depot at Bovington in Dorset, where we were sent on a weekend leave before flying back to Germany.

Chapter Fifteen

Mouse and I were separated as a matter of policy, though this didn't stop us remaining good pals. I went to B squadron, which on the day that I arrived was out on the ranges doing a tactical demonstration for visiting journalists and dignitaries. To my surprise, I was given command of a tank for that day. I didn’t really do much, except sit in the turret during the scripted mock attack, but the squadron OC was making a statement: fresh start and the chance to look for promotion.

This wasn’t as odd as it sounds. It was generally accepted that going to Military Prison straightened men out and prepared them for success in the Army. I knew this, but didn’t take advantage of the opportunity. Despite being twenty-six, I still wasn't thinking wisely or making good long-term decisions. So I volunteered for a job as barman in the sergeant’s and warrant officer’s mess, foolishly turning my back on the chance to make up for lost time with proper soldiering.

I was transferred to HQ squadron, with a job in the sergeant's mess alongside the mess corporal, Beastie Sutherland. Beastie had been bequeathed to 3RTR from another RTR regiment. His regiment had been disbanded by the government, to save money, during one of the shortsighted round of defence cuts some years earlier. We became good mates and later went on to work all sorts of dodges together.

Taking over the bar from another old soldier was a real learning curve. George Stocker knew all the dodges. He did a stock take with me. I had no idea how this should be done. He estimated the amounts left in open spirits bottle bye eye, and estimated quantities to cover up the many deficiencies he left with me. Eventually, I realised that I'd been turned over, but it was too late to prove anything. So, in time-honoured fashion, I gradually shifted the loss onto the mess account.

Another soldier was brought in to help, and we alternated days of work, except on mess function nights, when we both came in. The sergeants and warrant officers were mostly a good bunch, and I got on well with them. Quite a few were married, and they went home to married quarters and their wives when the regiment was in barracks. The single men decorated the bar most lunchtimes and every evening, Sergeant Pickering being one of them. Some, like the band sergeant major and the REME sergeant, became good friends of mine, and I enjoyed many evenings exchanging banter with them across the bar. The band sergeant major was always pulling my leg and making jokes about my Liverpool accent. One evening, in reply, I called him a daft bastard--not something a soldier would normally call a sergeant major. He just laughed. "Scouse," he said, "Don't you mean -'You're a daft bastard, *sir*!'"

At lunchtime, we opened the bar in the cellar so that the sergeants could have a drink whilst in working dress, as coveralls were banned in the mess. One of the staff sergeants' wives decided to make pasties in her home to be heated in a little oven and sold in the bar. There was no shortage of NAAFI pies, and the senior ranks enjoyed good pay and duty-free drink in the bar. So I couldn't see why she had to complicate my life with defrosting, heating, selling, and separately accounting for her bloody oggies. But she had the RSM's permission, so I had to grit my teeth and cooperate. That said, they were nice, so Beastie and I took to sharing one at break time whilst I was stocking up.

Naturally, we never paid for the pasties we ate, so when it came to accounting for them, we had a small cash crisis. Beastie came up with a bright idea. One of his jobs was buying extra food for the mess using the mess account. He suggested getting eggs and pickling vinegar on the mess account and selling pickled eggs to make money to pay for the pasties. We boiled the eggs in the sergeant's mess kitchen, very briefly pickled them in vinegar, and put them out on the bar. A pickled egg placed in a packet of crisps was a popular snack, and I soon made enough cash to pay our debts.

The mess had occasional formal evenings. All the mess members dined in the mess and then attended some sort of dance or disco afterwards. The sergeants and warrant officers wore mess dress, and the wives wore evening gowns. Lots of silver and regimental memorabilia decorated the tables. The whole thing looked very splendid and was undoubtedly lots of fun. But for Beastie and the waiters, plus myself working in the bar till stupid o'clock the next morning, it was a pain in the arse.

The mess decided to have a summer ball. They hired the civvy *schutzenhalle*, a big hall, a couple of miles away. So we had to transport the bar stock, tables and chairs, food, and so on. The evening followed the usual pattern. The single sergeants had an occasional dance, with some of the wives and various women dragged in from Paderborn. The married men spent the evening drinking and talking. Then, when most people had gone home, the hard drinkers sat around the near-empty hall, en route to oblivion. It all finished in the early hours of the morning, and everything (including some of the mess silver) was left unguarded and unattended. It shouldn't have happened like that, but it did.

Early next morning, Beastie and I decided to go out there and grab some bottles of wine for ourselves. The mess paid for everything that night. Whatever we grabbed was ours for free. But we had to get it before the stock take, which I was due to do later with the mess sergeant, Wayne Simpson. Beastie borrowed a car from a mate, and we drove out to the *schutzenhalle* and liberated a quantity of booze. Later in the day, we returned with Sergeant Simpson and some borrowed muscle from one of the squadrons, and discovered that we weren't the only ones to have paid an early and unofficial visit.

The mess owned a large model of a World War I tank. It was actually made of metal from one of the first tanks used during World War I - and it was missing. The model was probably quite valuable, but more importantly, it was a regimental heirloom and irreplaceable. Beastie and I, like most soldiers, wouldn't hesitate to nick bits and pieces from the stores or fiddle some drinks. As Kipling said, "Single men in barracks don't grow into plaster saints." But the tank was a different sort of theft, one that would have seemed criminal to us.

The military police carried out an investigation. A witness reported seeing a green car driving away from the scene. This was what we'd been driving. Wayne Simpson told us about it in his office, unaware of our visit to the hall to liberate some wine.

"Did they get the car registration number?" I asked with a sinking feeling. Luckily for us, they didn't. The investigation continued for a couple of days, but it was mainly concentrated amongst members of the sergeants' and warrant officers' mess, and didn't really become wider knowledge amongst the regiment. No one was ever caught, and the model tank wasn't found. But let me set the record straight: Beastie and I were not involved.

Working in the bar was generally pleasant enough. But problems came from one of the warrant officers, Squadron Sergeant Major Mick Soper. He had delusions of grandeur; unfortunately, he also had the rank to turn some of them into reality.

I had to wear a bowtie and white shirt on mess nights. I didn't like it much, but I could live with it, as it wasn't often I had to wear this uniform. But Soper persuaded the RSM that I should wear a bowtie every night, and it pissed me off to be dressed up like a flunkey. He wanted to make the mess increasingly formal - or pretentious, as it seemed to me. Instead of a soldier doing a temporary duty, I began to feel more like a servant.

Soper started to flex his muscles more and more. I think he was pissed with me because I was very friendly with a married

German lady, Hilde, who worked in the mess. Soper had his eye on her, but I got in the way. Life was getting too complicated, so I decided to move back to a sabre squadron.

Beastie had just transferred to A squadron, working in the G1098 store. This store held kit for issue on a temporary basis during exercises, such as sleeping bags and compasses and so on. Beastie put in a good word with the staff sergeant in charge. He was nicknamed Wobbly Gob, as he tended to chatter a lot. I got the job of arms storeman, taking over from one of the Armitage brothers, who was moving back to a tank troop

Being A squadron arms storeman was a cushy number. The armoury was on the ground floor of A (or accommodation) block, opposite Beastie's store. My job was to open up in the morning and issue weapons as and when needed. Every soldier had a personal weapon, the 9mm Sterling submachine gun, and it was his responsibility to keep it clean. I just had to liaise with the REME fitters for repairs and maintenance and account for the weapons as they were signed into the armoury.

The armoury held 7.62mm general purpose machine guns, two of which were fitted to each tank, one on the turret by the commander's hatch and the other coaxially with the main armament. I also had some rifles, some BREN guns, and a few Carl Gustav anti-tank weapons, plus the old .50 calibre ranging guns that Chieftain was fitted with before the introduction of laser rangefinders. As this lot didn't exactly keep me worked to death, I sometimes helped Beastie in the stores and did anything else that Wobbly Gob might dream up.

The squadron living accommodation was on the ground and first floor. Most of the top floor was empty, except for the squadron bar. Further down the long corridor, behind a locked dividing door, some sparsely furnished rooms were used as accommodation for soldiers from other regiments. Those troops were on a detached duty, guarding some high-security installation near Paderborn. My squadron was responsible for providing the bedding used by these lads, and also for checking for damage when they moved in or out every couple of weeks. I got involved in doing these checks, and it was to prove an excellent dodge later on, when I used it as an excuse to skive in barracks instead of going out on exercises.

The top floor was supposedly haunted. There were vague and unsubstantiated stories of wartime atrocities in the camp, though why the top floor, and not the other floors, should be haunted was glossed over. So no one from A squadron actually lived up there, despite it being full of empty rooms whilst the lads were living four to a room downstairs(though this wasn't considered especially crowded). Having been used by a Waffen SS regiment during the Second World War, I don't doubt that some nasty things might have happened there. But I wasn't superstitious, and it didn't put me off, so I moved my kit upstairs and had my own bedroom, bathroom, and toilet.

Something odd did actually happen to me one morning though. I had just got out of bed, and was standing by the door, when the door handle turned. I thought someone had come from downstairs and was messing around. So, quick as a flash, I opened the door and stepped outside. No one was there. I ran up and down the corridor and searched everywhere - but there just wasn't anyone around. I never did find an explanation for how my door handle turned. But I liked my new room, and I didn't let it bother me.

When the squadron was due to go on exercise, I came up with a bright idea. I suggested to the stores staff sergeant that I stay behind to administer the accommodation for the units moving in and out. To my surprise, he agreed. So when the squadron went away a few days later, I happily issued the weapons from the armoury and then went back to bed - it being 0100.

For the next two weeks there was little to do. I kept an eye on the accommodation, arranged a few minor repairs, and kept clear of wandering officers from RHQ, who, on seeing me, would try to co-opt me on some daft job. But since I was skilled at old soldiers' tricks, it didn't happen often. If necessary, I could move around unseen by diverting through attics or cellars.

There was a network of underground tunnels running throughout the camp and into the adjacent artillery barracks. Rumours abounded of underground installations left by the Nazis. Accompanied by a mate, I explored much of the tunnel network, once emerging through a small manhole in the middle of the cinema, covered in dust. We beat a hasty and final retreat, having discovered nothing more sinister than miles of tunnels for utilities and a few odd, but quite empty, chambers.

The squadron did an exchange visit with a unit from the US 7th Cavalry, an American heavy armour regiment based in southern Germany. I pulled the old stay-back trick to look after the top floor accommodation again, and was given the task of hosting some of the Yanks socially. Many of them were black, unlike the men in my regiment, which was strictly whites-only. Quite a few smoked cannabis. And I let some of them light up in my room, which was quiet and out of the way. I did try it myself but wasn't too impressed.

I'd settled back to regimental soldiering and was doing a good job in the armoury, which gained top marks in an inspection from visiting REME technicians. This pleased the OC to no end, and I was glad to be able to put my mistakes behind me. Or I was, until I got hungry one night after a few beers with one of the Armitage brothers (or at least I think that's who it was). We decided to get a sandwich from the NAAFI vending machines. The vending room was usually unlocked at night, but sometimes, for reasons unknown to us, the NAAFI civvy staff would lock the main entrance door. Never being one to let small details get in my way, I climbed up the front of the building and in through a small window about twelve feet above the door. I bought a couple of cheese rolls from the machine and climbed out again. But the barrack guard had been alerted by someone and was waiting. My mate legged it; I was nabbed, taken to the guardroom, and left in cells for the rest of the night.

The next morning, I received a message from the RSM. Until I revealed the identity of my mate, I would be kept in jail, regardless of how long that would be. I knew this wasn't an idle threat but nonetheless felt reluctant to inform. So I sent a message to Armitage via one of the soldiers going off guard duty, and, luckily, he decided to own up: That done, I was released from jail and sent back to the squadron. On the way out, I was given the two cheese rolls, though somehow they didn't seem so appealing at that moment. A few days later, I was on a charge in front of the OC. I can't remember my punishment - a fine, I think.

A few days later I was helping Beastie do stocktaking in one of the cellars. He had to send the squadron's supply of rum to a supply depot to be exchanged - all consumable stores were renewed periodically to ensure they were not tainted or damaged. These were war stocks, held to issue a tot of rum to each soldier in especially harrowing times, during combat. The rum was stored in big glass demi-johns. I held one up and looked at it longingly.

"Seems a shame to send it back untested," said Beastie.

"Certainly does," I said, "especially as this is probably the same as the old naval issue rum, and better than anything you can buy." So we came up with a plan.

The jars were corked and sealed to prevent tampering. We took a needle and a syringe and carefully inserted the needle down the side of the cork. Syringing the contents out was a lengthy but rewarding process that left us with a large amount of rum. We were also left with a sealed, but nonetheless empty, demi-john. Keeping the needle in place, we slowly refilled it with blackcurrant juice, adjusting the mixture as we went to make it look like rum. I'm not quite sure if this is what the Army means when it asks soldiers to show initiative.

Around this time, Wobbly Gob went off to a new job and, Staff Sergeant Graham Perkins took over as SQMS. He'd served on some sort of detached duty in the Middle East and had more medals than anyone else in the regiment. All credit to him, but he hung his No2 jacket behind the counter in the G1098 store, putting his medal ribbons on full display. This seemed a bit immodest, so Beastie and I relieved him of his regimental belt to discourage him from leaving his kit around. Beastie reckoned that Graham had a spare anyway: Sorry, Graham, I still have it if you want it back.

I'd liberated Graham's belt just before Cambrai Day. Every year, all the Royal Tank Regiments celebrate the anniversary of the battle of Cambrai. The battle took place on November 20' 1917, when British tanks broke through the German lines. This was the first time that tanks were used effectively in battle. It also happens to be my birthday.

The day starts with the sergeants, led by a piper, bringing gunsmoke (tea laced with rum) around the barracks to wake the lads up. Drinking starts immediately, as do the daft jokes. (I have an excellent photo of one officer's moped hoisted to the top of a flagpole.)

Dinner is a special event, accompanied by more alcohol and a speech from the colonel. The one I remember best had the lads on their feet cheering, as the colonel told us that artillery was no longer the key to winning battles—the new king of the battlefield was us, the tanks. The day progressed with more drinking and sports, including boxing matches in the gym, refereed by Corporal Colin Guppy. I can't remember anything about the boxing. I think the biggest cheer came for Guppy, *sans* underpants, whose trousers split as he was climbing over the ropes.

Mouse had been soldiering in a tank troop in one of the other squadrons. We were still pals, though not as close as before.

Whereas I'd settled down and was generally staying out of trouble, Mouse seemed to be courting it. Matters came to a head on Cambrai day. He was under punishment for something or other and was not allowed to go to the Cambrai Ball. Contrary to advice from me and a few of the lads, Mouse walked in and joined me. No one said anything, and we speculated whether or not his presence would go unnoticed. It was a drunken evening. I still have a photograph of us leaning back in our chairs, surrounded by beer, each holding a rose in our mouths. Why? I can't remember. The following day, Mouse was summoned to his squadron office. He was put on another charge and discharged from the Army, services no longer required. This is not as bad as a court martial and a dishonourable discharge, but leaving with SNLR on his record was a shame, though he seemed happy enough to be getting out. Mouse left with no punishment, no drama - just a seat on the bus to the airport and a final beer at lunchtime with me and his mate Adrian Roberts, otherwise known as 'chicken man' because of his previous civilian job slaughtering chickens. Looking back, I can't help feeling some responsibility and regret - for Mouse leaving the Army - not the chickens!

Meanwhile, my three-year engagement in the Army was coming to an end. I was asked to reenlist but decided against it. I looked for something that would offer me a good civilian career. What went through my mind when I chose nursing, I can't for the life of me recall. But to help my application, I bought two books on human biology and sat a GCE O level exam.

My own departure from the regiment was a subdued business. Wayne Simpson, the mess sergeant, gave me a lift to the station to get a train back to England. I'd had a quiet drink the day before with one or two pals and a routine interview with the new colonel. He said that I was welcome to come back to the regiment and could contact him directly. I had no intention of doing so, but I nonetheless appreciated his words.

Chapter Sixteen

On February 28, 1982, I was transferred to the reserve. It felt odd to be a civilian again. I moved to my mother's house which was now in Newton Abbot and spent copious amounts of time and money at the Cider Bar on East Street.

Mother had been a diabetic for years. Now she also had Cushing's Syndrome, a pituitary disorder that necessitated the removal of her adrenal glands. From then on she took steroids, and her health continued to deteriorate. I was still very close to her and tried to be supportive. With hindsight, I can see that the financial and material help I gave wasn't what she really needed. She was lonely, and she wanted companionship. I did spend time with her, but I wish now that I'd spent more.

My sister Pam had joined the Army a year earlier as a driver. She married an infantryman, who turned out to be a selfish, philandering idiot. Soon, I found a flat in Exeter and then a job in

Exminster Hospital working in the laundry. The work was hard, but the people I worked with made it good fun.

My application for nurse training was accepted by Southmead Hospital in Bristol, and in November 1983, I packed my kit and moved into the nurses' home. Living as one of very few males in accommodation full of nurses must be every young man's dream. I hadn't had too many girlfriends whilst in the forces, but now I made up for lost time with a string of short-term relationships.

Two years went by quickly. I qualified as an enrolled nurse and then worked for a further couple of years on a surgical ward. Eventually, I got fed up with nursing and decided to move on. By now I was living with another nurse, Karen, who I'd met whilst working on J Ward at Southmead Hospital. I took a job as an insurance salesman but left after a few weeks. They wanted me to push my friends and family to buy insurance - no way.

Then I got a job with Everaids. They only made one product: a powered wheelchair. It was revolutionary in design, allowing a disabled child to be carried either standing or sitting. The company was expanding and looking for a representative for the north of England, so off I went with Karen and bought a house in Doncaster.

It really was a fantastic wheelchair, but it cost as much as many people would pay for a good secondhand car, and it wasn't funded by the NHS. Nonsensical sales projections, based on disability percentages amongst the population, didn't equate to real sales. I could see the writing on the wall, so I left and reluctantly went back to nursing, taking a job in Doncaster Royal Infirmary. Sometime after this, Everaids ceased trading.

My relationship went bust too, and Karen and I sold the house and went our separate ways. We'd been together a couple of years and it upset me a lot, but I got over it. I found a job at Winford Orthopaedic Hospital on an orthopaedic surgical ward. I also attempted SAS selection with E squadron of the 21st SAS regiment. This was a Territorial Army unit based at Raglan Barracks in Newport, South Wales.

Reserve SAS selection was a scaled-down version of the regular army SAS training. This was done over a number of weekends. The first weekend was quite surreal, with assault courses and navigation around tunnel complexes. The oddest thing was running along a lane at Pontrilas training area and coming upon a passenger jet aeroplane used in anti-terrorist training stood on bricks in a field.

Subsequent weekends consisted of increasing intensity tabbing - long timed hikes - in the Black Mountains and the Brecon Beacons. We would start off on Friday evening from a checkpoint, carrying a massively overloaded bergan (backpack), and have to navigate to the next checkpoint on some mountain ridge or wherever. We went from checkpoint to checkpoint, and as we didn't know how long we had, we always moved at absolute top speed. Unlike regular SAS selection, we did at least know it had to come to an end by Sunday night. It doesn't sound much, though men have died of exposure and exhaustion whilst doing it. But you had to be good to even get a place on the selection course, and it tested stamina, determination, and motivation to their absolute limits. Many trained soldiers didn't get through the initial screening to try selection. Of those that did, the overwhelming majority failed (because the standards were so high), as I did on my first attempt and again on the second attempt a year later.

In March 1989, I joined 219 (TA) Field Hospital, which had a detachment in Keynsham, Bristol. Lots of the TA (Royal Army Medical Corps) soldiers were qualified civilian doctors and nurses. I was very happy with 219; I made lots of good friends and enjoyed the training weekends and annual two-week exercise in Germany. I did well in that unit and was promoted. They didn't want me to leave. But, yet again, I felt the urge to do something radically different. So I joined the Royal Air Force.

Part Three: The Royal Air Force

Chapter Seventeen

The RAF has its own infantry regiment, imaginatively named the RAF Regiment. Its role is the ground defence of RAF bases in the UK and abroad. I went into the recruiting office in Bristol and said I was interested in joining. The familiar process of military recruiting commenced, but when they discovered that I was a trained nurse, they persuaded me to change my application to nursing.

It didn't take too much persuasion. Joining as a nurse meant not having to do trade training, and I would start with the rank of senior aircraftsman (SAC) instead of aircraftsman. Nurses were also on a higher technical pay band, so it was a good deal financially. But it was a shortsighted decision on my part. I was fed up with nursing *per se*,and I missed out on the chance to do something new - something that might have retained my interest and enthusiasm in the long term.

They sent me to London for a specialist interview with a nursing branch squadron leader. She warned me that RAF hospitals were far less busy that the NHS, and there would be times when I had nothing to do.

"Are you alright with that?" she asked.

"No problem," I replied. "I'll be able to get away when it's quiet and play sport."

That's how things would have worked in the Army. I made assumptions that she should have corrected. Later, I found that no matter how quiet a ward was, and no matter how many people were stood around bored with nothing to do, no one was ever allowed to get away and do anything else.

Back in Bristol, I took the recruiting tests and medicals. Then I was given a date to report to RAF Swinderby for recruit training. Everyone had to go through this six-week training, even those who had been in the services before - including two lads I was to meet later: Malcolm, an ex-RAF bandsman, plus an ex-paratrooper who earned my undying admiration when he had a sense of humour failure and punched a PTI who beasted him too much in the gym.

A couple of years earlier, my sister had divorced her husband and moved to Doncaster, just before Mother passed away. Now Pam let me use her house in Urban Road, Hexthorpe, as my home base when on leave.

Early in January 1990, I threw my kit into my Nissan Cherry and drove down to RAF Swinderby to report to the guardroom.

Having gone through basic training before with both the Navy and Army, I knew what to expect. The terminology was different, but the process much the same. The recruits were divided into 'flights' instead of troops, under the charge of a flight sergeant, instead of a sergeant. The accommodation was similar, with lots of ten-man rooms in accommodation blocks.

Things followed a predictable pattern. We all got to know each other. Friendships were made, and a few animosities, too. We were taken to the stores and issued with kit. Looking after kit was simple compared to my experiences in the Navy two decades earlier. For instance, shirts didn't have to be folded; they could be left on hangers in your locker. We were also allowed to keep personal items locked away separately in a large overhead cupboard,which didn't get inspected.

There was a daily kit muster, with bed blocks and kit layed out on beds, but compared to what I'd been used to, it was easy. It took me no time at all to get my kit sorted out so that I could swiftly lay it out on my bed each morning. The rooms and corridors and bathrooms still had to be cleaned and polished, but, again, not to the standards I'd been used to.

Each day followed familiar patterns of parade drill, lectures, and physical instruction. The RAF's foot drill is pretty much like the Army's, so that was easy. Initially, the physical training was mostly cross-country runs, which I was fit enough to enjoy. After a couple of weeks, however, that changed. We spent more time in the gym for the usual nonsense of jumping over wooden boxes, so I reported myself sick with a story about pulling my Achilles tendon and was given an "excused PT" chit that lasted till the end of basic training. You'd have never gotten away with that in the Army.

The flight was about forty strong. Malcolm Goodman, an ex-RAF corporal, was given the job of recruit flight leader. I was given the job of recruit deputy flight leader. It wasn't a real promotion. It was like being a bloody school prefect - just a temporary thing during basic training, a nuisance that I should have turned down.

Malcolm and I had to make sure everyone was in the right place at the right time and march the flight around camp to wherever. We also supervised the cleaning of the accommodation block each evening in preparation for the inspection the next morning. It wasn't a difficult task, but some of the lads rebelled and we had to push them a lot. This made me fairly unpopular, which didn't worry me in the least.

Malcolm proved to be a good mate. Sometimes in the evening, after getting everyone sorted with their cleaning jobs, we'd go down to the NAAFI for a beer. He didn't drink a lot, though, and I'd often go on my own.

Regardless of the differing specialist training which recruits did later, everyone shared initial recruit training. The best part of this basic training was ground defence, run by the RAF Regiment corporals. This consisted of weapons training, some basic infantry skills, plus NBC training. I'd done it before, but getting out on the ranges and firing the SLR again was good fun, and I managed to earn myself a marksman's badge.

Unlike basic training with the other services, we were allowed to go on weekend leave. I couldn't believe it when I heard this. But sure enough, every Friday evening at five o'clock, I was able to jump in the car and go home till Sunday evening. Pam was in a TA infantry battalion—C Company, Yorkshire Volunteers. On my second weekend in the RAF, I joined her. We went out with the TA, spending Saturday and Sunday running around the woods in Catterick (Yorkshire), with a GPMG machine gun and a belt of ammunition, setting up ambushes and other bits of fun.

RAF basic training was easy, but sometimes the recruits made it difficult. Instead of getting to sleep at night, some of them would run around, playing childish games and making a racket. Malcolm or I would put a stop to it, but it was a bloody nuisance that I kept losing sleep over. My standard of physical fitness actually dropped by the time recruit training finished. Too much to eat, too much to drink, and less physical activity, like running, than I'd become used to.

Training finished after six weeks, followed by a passing out parade and a fly past by a Tornado jet fighter. The families of the graduating Flights sat around the edge of the parade square. The visiting senior officer inspected the graduating flights and presented prizes. The whole parade then marched around to the sound of the RAF band, saluting the reviewing officer on the dais before marching off the parade ground.

My flight led the parade, with hundreds of men following on and taking their timing from us. Our drill instructor departed from the normal routine. A body of men is lined up with the tallest on the end and the shortest in the middle, giving an even and uniform appearance as a whole. This would put my diminutive self firmly in the middle of the ranks. But for the previous six weeks, I had often been the right hand marker during parade training, as I could already drill to a fairly high standard.

I pointed out the very obvious anomaly of myself at five feet and four inches on the end, with the six-foot-plus guys following on behind me. But the decision was made to forget sizing; because the whole parade followed us, the right-hand marker from our flight had to get it right. I still have a video of the parade. I'm leading, carrying a rifle and bayonet almost as tall as myself - and looking good, too, I might modestly add.

After basic finished in late February 1990, everyone was posted to various air stations for trade training, apart from Malcolm and me. He went straight to an RAF Band, and I received a posting direct to duties at an RAF Hospital. The RAF only had two hospitals left then: Wroughton and Halton. An admin sergeant asked me which one I wanted to get posted to, and I chose Wroughton. So it came as no great surprise to be posted to Halton, where I reported to the guardroom as instructed.

Becky L. arrived at the guardroom at the same time. I knew her vaguely from Swinderby. She was also a nurse, and in the same intake as me, though in one of the female flights. We went through the joining routine together, where we got accommodation and bedding and so on. In the evening, we met for a drink in the hospital social club, and the next morning went to the different wards to which we'd been allocated.

I was sent to a renal unit without patients. I spent the next few days stood around, bored witless. I knew that if I made a fuss, something would be found for me to do - something tedious, to discourage me from rocking the boat. So I kept quiet, as I was only on the renal ward for a few days until the start of a two-week first aid course that all nurses new to the RAF had to do. At this time, I still had the option to leave under the notice agreement, but I convinced myself it would all be fine once I was doing a permanent job.

The fist aid course was first rate, run by a corporal called Ian who made it fun whilst still imparting knowledge. When the course finished, I was sent to my permanent job on Ward 6, a mixed ward doing a mixture of minor surgery, ENT, and ophthalmic. Basically, it was all simple routine surgery and very, very undemanding.

It all went downhill from there. In the NHS, I'd been a clinical Grade E nurse, which meant I had a management and supervisory role, often in charge of a very busy surgical ward. Now I wasn't even allowed to give out the medications.

Enrolled nurses were used as little more than untrained assistants. Frankly, I couldn't understand why the RAF bothered to recruit them. All the extended roles and interesting work was done by the registered nurses, who were either commissioned officers or junior technicians, senior in rank to the enrolled nurses whose training was a year shorter. The RAF enforced a policy that no enrolled nurses were to be promoted above the rank of Senior Aircraftsman. There were some who had joined years earlier and were now corporals or flight sergeants, but that was no consolation to me.

The only people with even less responsibility than me were the medical assistants, otherwise known as care bears. At least for them it was only a short-term position, before they went on to an operational air station and did proper jobs. Denied all responsibility and only allowed to do simple tasks way below my competence levels, it wasn't long before I was thoroughly fed up and full of contempt for the Air Force.

On the worst days, a little group of ENs and care bears would stand around the ward in the afternoon with nothing to do. We still had to appear busy, regardless of reality; doing nothing was frowned upon. My assumption that such time would be a window of opportunity to get away for a couple of hours for a cross-country run or some other sport proved to be foolish. You might have been able to arrange something like that as a one off, but in general, standing around and pretending to be busy was the order of the day.

I spoke to people and tried to get a posting to an operational air station. I tried to volunteer for SAS selection as a way of getting away for a while, but at thirty-seven was considered too old. I'd signed on with the RAF for six years, but by now I was so incredibly bored that I applied for a discretionary early discharge. It was accepted, and though my pay was reduced, it was worth it. I now only had one and a half years during which to be bored witless.

Meanwhile, in the Middle East, the situation between Iraq and the Gulf States was going from bad to worse. The Gulf States had been sheltering themselves from Iranian fundamentalism behind Iraq, which had fought a long and bloody war against Iran and the ayatollahs. Iraqi debts in 1998 amounted to forty billion dollars, much of which was now owed to Kuwait.

Iraq was in deep debt, with an economy suffering badly from falling oil prices. The Emir of Kuwait refused to reduce oil output and, in doing so, push prices up. He wouldn't lend any more money, and he insistently demanded that Saddam Hussein make debt repayments.

Saddam felt that Iraq had paid for its loans with Iraqi blood and said something to the effect that the Emir was an ungrateful shit. Like most of my colleagues, this was only of passing interest to me: Though it was to grab everyone's attention well enough later in the year.

Chapter Eighteen

I had a couple of weeks' leave due and felt the urge to do something exciting. I'd always wanted to see Mount Everest, so I decided to put together my own little expedition. Someone suggested that I see the group captain in command of the hospital and request an extra week's leave for adventure training purposes. Adventure training didn't tend to figure in the hospital's activities, but I thought it worth asking and requested an interview. To my surprise, the group captain actually gave me two weeks extra leave, which I was very grateful for.

The officer in charge of my ward was Flight Lieutenant Wroe, a registered nurse. He was a good guy, but he didn't want anyone on the ward upsetting the status quo, and I was a nuisance to him. I'd already had a week away when I volunteered for the Nijmegan March in Holland - a hundred-mile march with thousands of military and civilian participants. It had been a great week, and I became good mates with the apprentices from the RAF College, as well as Dave, the flight sergeant dental technician who led us.

Flight Lieutenant Wroe, or Fish Egg, as I'd nicknamed him, put his best face to my latest venture. He couldn't prevent it now that I had official sanction, and I took a flight to Kathmandu in Nepal. My preparations were basic but thorough. I had a good insurance policy to cover the cost of helicopter evacuation by the Royal Nepalese Air Force if I should have an accident. I had maps of the Himalayas and a decent first aid kit. I wore Danner boots, well broken in from the Nijmegan Marches, and had a knife and a good sleeping bag. Then, I took a flight to Nepal.

At the Kathmandu airport, I jumped into a *tuk-tuk* for a ride to the city. The little motorised three-wheeled taxi spewed out vast clouds of black fumes as I clung to my bergan in the back. I found a guesthouse for the night, and then went to a government office to buy a trekking permit for the Solu-Khumbu (Everest)region. In the afternoon, I visited the temples in Durbar Square. The following morning, I took the bus to Jiri, which is where the roads finish and the walking begins.

Walking was easy in navigational terms, with a clearly defined footpath and occasional travellers to give directions if needed. It was the physical difficulty that hit me. The Himalayas start where European mountains leave off. Even on the lower regions, the altitude and reduced oxygen take their toll.

By the end of the first day's trek, I was well and truly knackered. I stopped in a hilltop clearing. There were pine trees all around and a soft mist had gathered. It looked more like Wales than Asia. I went into the only building, a simple two-storey wooden rest house. My priority was a wooden bucket shower and vast quantities of food, and I had *dall*, a lentil and vegetable dish I was to eat on a daily basis. That night, I slept like the dead, and I woke the next morning feeling refreshed. To lighten my load, I went through my kit and threw away as much as I could, cutting my towel in half and even cutting off the edges of the maps.

I trekked on, and though I enjoyed the mountain scenery, I found it hard going even carrying a reduced load. At lunchtime, at a tiny hamlet called Kenja, I did what many people do and hired a porter. If I'd had more time, I could have taken things more slowly on my own and gradually acclimatised, but getting back late wasn't an option. So I hired Khalu, a little guy who quite literally dropped everything and signed on with me for one hundred rupees a day.

A teashop owner translated for me, saying that Khalu was delighted. Getting work as a porter was sought-after but difficult, as most of the hiring was done in Kathmandu. We spent the next few days walking higher and higher across the mountains. We passed Lukla at nine thousand feet. This is where most people started their trek, flying in to the precarious dirt airstrip that ran along the top of a ridge. Seeing wrecked aeroplanes that hadn't quite got it right, I was glad I took the hard way.

The other benefit of walking was that I got mountain fit. My legs were stronger, and I gradually got used to the lower concentration of oxygen. It's best to adjust slowly, as pulmonary and cerebral oedema can be lethal at high altitudes. Rapid ascent causes fluid to collect in the cells. The first symptoms are headaches and shortness of breath as fluid collects around the lungs and brain. Unless you descend rapidly, the next stage is coughing up blood and a passage into unconsciousness and death. I hoped to avoid that particular fate.

We climbed another couple of thousand feet and reached Namche Bazaar. I had tea with the Tibetanmonks at a monastery I passed as I headed northwards. Eventually, I reached Pheriche, a tiny village of stone huts and the last real shelter before Everest. Very early the next morning, I trekked up to a mountain overlooking Everest base camp. I stopped on the way for a cup of tea at a tiny stone hut at Gorak Shep (Crow's Death), a bleak, rocky, almost lunar-looking landscape.

Ascending Kala Pattar, a spur of Pumori, at eighteen thousand feet was more of a steep walk than a climb, but to put it in perspective, it was still a couple of thousand feet higher than the Matterhorn. The views were breathtaking.

I sat on a rock, looking at Everest base camp in the valley below and at the towering bulk of Everest above me. Then, in the midst of this almost mystical moment, an Irishman appeared from behind a rock. I snapped back to reality, we chatted for a few minutes, and I made my way back to Pheriche. Khalu was sat in a little stone hut, attempting to break the Nepalese noodle-eating record at my expense. The little guy was more than welcome. He was just as short as me but slightly built, without any obvious muscle. Yet he'd carried my bergan on the highest trek in the world without a word of complaint.

The return trek was easier, as I was really fit by then. At Namche Bazaar, I paid Khalu off. I gave him the money I owed him, plus what he would have earned if he'd carried my kit back to Kenja. I carried my own bergan from then on, as a soldier should, and eventually reached Jiri.

The bus from Jiri to Kathmandu was just as uncomfortable and overloaded as it had been on the trip there, except that this time the bald tyres didn't get a puncture. I had a couple of days before my flight and did some serious drinking in Tom and Jerry's bar. I also made the mistake of eating some ice cream. The result was the Kathmandu quick step or Delhi belly. Whatever you choose to call it, it wasn't nice.

Back at Halton, everyone expected me to settle down quietly. Fish Egg told me that I should be grateful for having had time off to trek to Everest and should not ask for anything else. I was appreciative, though sport and adventure training is meant to be part of service life for those who want it. But I was still bored witless and felt under-utilised in my work until an unexpected ally came to my rescue. I doubt if my situation was on Saddam's mind, but the Iraqi invasion of Kuwait, though a tragedy for the Kuwaiti people, was my escape route from Halton.

Saddam Hussein demanded that the Kuwaitis cancel the loans owed them and take action to stabilise oil prices. The Iraqis also had a longstanding claim on Kuwaiti territory, going back to the breakup of the Ottoman Empire. Internationally, no one gave their claim much credence. But the Iraqis did, or at least they pretended to, though what they really wanted were Kuwaiti oil fields.

There was a final meeting between the two countries. The Emir of Kuwait made some remark to the effect that if the Iraqis wanted money they should send their women out on to the streets. This was a dumb thing to say; though I doubt they need me to point it out at this stage. Saddam took this as a personal insult against his mother, which it was meant to be. He said, "The Emir will not be sleeping in his palace tonight," and launched his army at Kuwait.

The Kuwaiti army had around sixteen thousand men. The Iraqis attacked with three Republican Guard divisions, with an immediate backup force of somewhere between ninety and one hundred thousand men, and Kuwait was well and truly defeated.

At Halton, we speculated about our involvement, but routine carried on as normal. A few medical assistants went out to join small detachments in Saudi Arabia and Bahrain. I continued to do nothing remotely useful on Ward 6. A friend came back from one of the detachments and warned us that the RAF medical services' commitment in the Middle East would likely be increased. It was a fairly safe prediction.

Whilst all this was going on, I was frantically worried that I'd be left behind to stand around the ward, fetching and caring for bloody civilian patients. Civilians also used the RAF hospital, and some of them seemed to think we were there as servants.

Some people sent out to the Gulf to join units were keen enough to go. Some were not, and would have been happy staying at Halton. I watched in frustration and then came up with one of my bright ideas: I would write to the director of the RAF Medical Services and tell him how stupid the situation was. A medical clerk in the administrative office found the name and address and discreetly passed it on to me.

So I wrote my letter, which went something to the following effect: "Dear Air Vice Marshal, I'm qualified and keen to go to the war, so please use me instead of leaving me wasting my time achieving nothing in Halton."

Writing something like this was totally against all service protocol and would undoubtedly bring the wrath of the gods down on my head. Nonetheless, I set off to the hospital, intending to post it on the way. As I was running a bit late, I changed my mind and decided to post it later, after tea break. At tea break, I walked out to go to the post box and bumped into the squadron leader deputy matron.

“Good news,” she said. “I know how desperate you are to go, and so your name is on the list for the formation of a field hospital to be deployed to the Gulf.”

"Brilliant! Thank you very much, ma'am," I replied, thinking how lucky it was that I’d delayed posting that stupid letter.

For the last couple of months, I’d been going out with an RAF nurse called Krista. She wasn’t joining us at the field hospital, and she took my impending departure badly. I’d been having second thoughts and had decided to end things anyway, though not quite in the way that it actually transpired.

A couple of good mates were also nominated for No4 RAF War Hospital: SAC Stuart Leverton and SAC Tim Hill, who was otherwise known as Mallet, after some crazy children's television presenter. Tim was crazed himself, and always ready with a joke to cheer things up.

We were sent for ten days' nuclear, biological, and chemical defence (NBC) training at Saighton Camp, a TA (reserve soldier) camp just outside of Chester. We were divided into groups, under the supervision of a NBC instructor, with my group having a female sergeant from the TA. It was unusual to have a TA soldier teaching regulars. But regardless, she was an excellent instructor.

Saddam, or Sad-Ham as we sometimes called him, had stockpiles of nerve agents such as Sarin. He'd already used this on the Kurds, to awful effect. So we took the training very seriously. That's to say we made sure we learnt it thoroughly, though we weren't averse to messing around and having a laugh about it.

We'd all had NBC training before, but not as intense as this. We checked our respirators, or gas masks, to see that they fitted and didn't leak. We practiced *ad infinitum,* changing canisters and drinking in a contaminated environment and so on. We did all the immediate action drills and got into our charcoal-impregnated protective suits in record time. Then, the instructor would shout "Gas, gas, gas!"-- the warning of chemical or biological contamination. I'd pull the respirator from the bag slung around my waist and put it on, repeating "Gas, gas, gas!" in a muffled voice through the mask. The next step was to put on the trousers, followed by the protective jacket and then the over-boots and rubber gloves.

The jacket had a hood, which I pulled over my head and sealed around the face of my respirator. Then we worked in pairs, checking that each other's suits were fitted properly, and blotting fuller's earth around the respirator to mop up imaginary drops of mustard gas or whatever.

Finished, we'd stand there looking like google-eyed aliens. Then we'd go through the drills, again and again. None of these drills were especially difficult, but being slow or getting it wrong might prove lethal in the future. So we kept at it and learnt how to survive this especially rotten sort of warfare.

Nerve agent pre-treatment sets (NAPS tablets) were issued to everyone. These give a limited degree of resistance when taken before exposure to nerve gas. We were also given auto-injectors, with which to inject ourselves with atropine, an antidote to nerve agents, should we have the symptoms of poisoning. To prove to us that it worked, the RAF showed a film of a monkey strapped in a chair inside a chamber contaminated with nerve gas. The poor bloody monkey writhed in agony. Then, technicians dressed in protective suits injected it with atropine. The monkey started to recover immediately, I'm glad to say.

A minute drop of nerve agent on the skin is enough to kill. To add to the fun, it's also lethal if inhaled or ingested. The symptoms are about as unpleasant as it gets. It starts with a nasal discharge, excessive salivation, and a tightening of the chest. At this stage, you need to inject yourself with atropine or the symptoms very, very rapidly progress to difficulty breathing, blurred vision, and irritation of the eyes. This is followed by involuntary urination, defecation, and then death. All of this takes just minutes, unless the atropine injections (which must be repeated every fifteen minutes) reverse it.

To further emphasise the seriousness of it all, we were shown a film of the aftermath of Saddam's nerve gas attack on Halabjah. Around two years earlier, in March 1988, the Iraqis had regained territory previously lost to Iran. Saddam decided to teach his newly liberated Kurdish citizens a lesson in loyalty—something he felt they had shown a lack of. So he directed his cousin Ali Hassan al-Majid to organise an attack on the civilian population using chemical weapons, resulting in around five thousand civilian deaths and another ten thousand casualties.

There were lots of other unpleasant ways to die, and we were given multiple injections of vaccines, including anthrax, the plague, and botulinum.

Anthrax survives well in the sunlight and is an ideal biological warfare agent for the desert; it is also fatal. Plague comes in a number of varieties, from the treatable to the fatal, whilst botulinum toxin has a survival rate of about 30 percent, given swift medical treatment. The vaccinations were voluntary, but we trusted our senior officers and the Ministry of Defence, and so far as I know, everyone had them.

Saddam also had many other ways to kill or maim us including mustard gas of World War I notoriety. But you shouldn't think that this depressed us. On thecontrary, as servicemen have done since time immemorial, we went out and had a good time whenever possible.

Medical units are inevitably mixed, and I met up with a young female medical assistant called S. at Saighton Camp. I should have been straight with Krista and told her, but she found out through the medical services bush telegraph. I treated her badly - something I now regret.

Before the NBC course finished, two army officers who had just returned from the Middle East brought us together and gave a briefing. They stood up in front of a large map and proceeded to indicate strength and capability of Iraqis. It made for sobering listening.

Iraqi military expenditure in 1998 had been 41 percent of the country's GDP. It had the third-largest army in the world, with a conscript defence force of one million personnel and a nominal total of two million, if you included all the armed forces and reservists. Conscript armies don't always have the best reputation, compared to motivated volunteer professionals. But the Iraqis had endured a decade of bloody trench warfare against the Iranians and were experienced and battle hardened. Much of their equipment was Soviet and technologically less advanced than ours, but it was still an impressive array and numerically far superior to the Allied forces deployed to the Gulf. They had seven armoured/mechanised divisions, forty-two infantry divisions, six Republican Guard divisions, three Special Forces brigades and two Surface-to-Surface Missile brigades.

To add to the fun, the Iraqis had the world's sixth-largest air force, equipped with a mixture of Soviet and western aeroplanes. There were seventy Mig 23/27s and sixty-one French Mirage F1s, thirty Hunters, thirty Su-7Bs, fifty Su-20s, plus some air defence squadrons.

A briefing from the CO at No4 RAF War Hospital, Wing Commander Davies, followed the briefing from the army officers. We were given all sorts of information about our role in the forthcoming war. But the subject of personal weapons caused the biggest consternation and uproar I ever saw in my time in HM Forces. It was simple - most of us just wouldn't have a weapon. The result was general outrage, and I was one of the most outraged.

Medics aren't sent anywhere with the intention of getting into combat. But in a war zone, anything can happen, and medics are entitled under the Geneva Convention to defend themselves. But they need a weapon with which to do it. Apparently there would be a few rifles and submachine guns. These would be issued to members of the RAF regiment band, who were coming with us, as their wartime role is to work with the medical services.

I was keen to do my duty, yet I was also well aware that things often go wrong, and safe areas become danger zones very quickly. Take, for instance, the atrocities at the British Army hospital in Singapore: during World War II, the Japanese bayoneted the wounded and the doctors, and then raped the female nurses before bayoneting them too.

I didn't have unquestioning faith in our allies, either. The Korean War started badly, and we came close to defeat in the initial stages; the war in Vietnam ended badly too. This was how my mind was working at the time. It brings a wry smile to my face now. But hindsight is a wondrous thing; it felt serious enough then.

I went to the CO and pointed out that I was well trained in fighting skills, especially by RAF standards. I suggested that I should be one of the few issued with a rifle, in case fighting broke out around the hospital. He said that if I was that bothered about it all, I could have the Browning 9mm pistol with which he'd been issued. I knew he was fobbing me off, and our first meeting ended with a mutually poor opinion of each other - something that would be totally reversed before it was all over.

It was December by then, and we were all sent on two weeks' embarkation leave. I went to stay with my sister, Pam. Going to war, even as a medic, brings out some serious discussions within families. I was expecting something akin to a disaster, and I thought my own death a real possibility. Of course, we didn't know then how one-sided the body count was going to be.

The issue of deploying without a weapon continued to worry me, and I was sceptical of the CO's promise to give me his pistol. I discussed it all with Pam, going over festive topics such as how I would like to be buried if my body was recovered. I went to Malcolm Foy, a firm of solicitors in Doncaster, to make a will and explained the urgency of the matter, although it took them so long that the war was nearly over before I got to sign the completed will form. Then, having made the preparations I could, I got on with enjoying the remainder of my leave.

Christmas 1990 was lovely. My nieces Jennifer and Danielle were still children, and it was a special family day for us. We sat down for a traditional festive dinner, and then we listened to the Queen's speech. I can't remember her exact words, but they left me feeling sure that we were about to embark on a bloody war, not on a game of bluff and brinkmanship, as some commentators had suggested.

The following day after lunch, Pam drove me to a motorway junction on the A1M. I met up with John Wilson, a flight sergeant from Tadcaster. He gave me a lift back to Halton.

Later that night, I caught one of the buses to RAF Brize Norton for the flight to Muharraq, in Bahrain. We flew in a Kuwaiti Airlines wide-bodied jet - a nice a way to fly to war, except for the lack of alcohol.

The following morning, we landed at Muharraq. The airfield was a hive of activity. RAF Tornado and Jaguar fighters stood in rows awaiting takeoff. A huge USAF Galaxy transport was disgorging equipment. There was air and ground activity everywhere.

We climbed into buses, but instead of going to the hospital site, they took us to a commandeered hotel in Bahrain city. It wasn't exactly luxurious, but it was head and shoulders above what we'd expected. We stayed there for the next few days, taking advantage of the opportunity to have a wild New Year's Eve.

This was all too good to last, of course, and a few days later we moved to a compound near the old mud-walled fort at Arad. Again, to my surprise, the accommodation was pretty good, and the food, cooked by Indian chefs, was even better. The hospital complex itself was a few miles away.

We took over from an Army unit, 22 Field Hospital. They had put up a hundred-bed facility consisting of tents. There was also a sealed unit made of chemical and gas-proof fabric, with facilities inside where we could operate on casualties as they came in from the battlefield. This was called Colpro, short for collective protection. It maintained a higher air pressure inside, drawing air through big filters that removed chemical or biological warfare agents and nuclear fallout particles.

My first priority was to find the CO and bend his ear about weapons. I found him in a little office surrounded by the usual administrative people. Everyone seemed to be milling around and making a lot of racket, whilst not appearing to actually do anything useful.

I asked about the personal weapon I was supposedly getting, and - surprise, surprise - it wasn't going to materialise. I opened my next statement with the phrase, "Sir, with respect . . ."

"With respect" is said when disagreeing with an officer. It implies certain things, unstated but understood, that allow you to stretch the boundaries of argument. It's an unspoken acknowledgement that you will not push beyond unacceptable limits.

The CO looked down at me from his considerable six-foot-plus bulk. "Widders, there's really no need for you to be armed." He continued with reassurances that nothing could get through the airborne might of the RAF, and that the RAF Regiment would defend us on the ground and so on.

"Sir, with respect, I don't give a fish's tit about all that," I said tactfully. "I just want to be armed, in case things go wrong."

He heard me out, but I could see that he thought I was just panicking. "There's going to be a QRF [quick reaction force], which will be armed, and I'll make sure that you get put on it. Okay?"

"Yes, sir," I said grudgingly - and sceptically.

A couple of days later, I went and found the station warrant officer (the position is a bit like an army RSM) and had a go at him about weapons. To my surprise, the CO had actually seen him about putting me on the QRF. I was a little happier with the situation then. But of course, it never bloody happened, which shouldn't have come as any great shock, really.

I had concerns, but in general, things were good. As Arab countries go, the place was quite liberal, with alcohol, music, etc. I wrote to my family. I told them how safe we were and how the natives thought we were so wonderful, and that there wasn't any terrorist threat. We were probably in the best location in the Gulf. But like everyone else, I wanted to get in, do the job, and come back home.

In war, one of the most important items is ammunition. RAF regulations state that the "personal weapon for medical personnel is the self loading pistol (SLP), which personnel are to be in possession of, if deployed." But I still didn't have one, so ammo wasn't too big a concern to me.

Welfare is another important issue. Field Marshal Montgomery said that "the best form of welfare for soldiers is training." I thought so, too, and took part in all the training that was going, and sometimes organised my own. For instance, I sat with my friend Karla Weekes, and we practiced putting venflons, needles used to put intravenous fluids into wounded soldiers, in each other.

One very real welfare issue was mail. If I had to choose one factor as the key to keeping up morale, it was letters from home. I received a parcel from Pam, with tins of my favourite foods, some biscuits, and a little bottle of rum. It wasn't that we were short of much, but it was comforting and reassuring to get those bits and pieces from home. Pam was bringing up two children without any help from their father. She didn't have money to throw around, and the parcel and the many letters she sent were something special that I will forever remain thankful for.

Pam wrote to tell me that she had read in the newspapers that Saddam Insane had a biological warfare capability, with anthrax and botulinum. She was right, too, though I didn't make too much of it in my reply. Biological warfare was a very real possibility, and the RAF started offering more vaccinations during the next few days. Queuing up for vaccinations wasn't a problem, though. I had plenty of time, as there weren't any wounded and most of the equipment hadn't arrived, anyway. I thought that the organisation was a total disaster, but aside from all that, I was fit and well and happy.

Then the Iraqis started firing Scud missiles. Being a bit of a blunt instrument, they were aimed in the vague direction of the Allied airfields, one of which was right next door to us. The Scud came to the Iraqis via the Soviets, who developed them from German V-2 rockets fired at England during World War II. It was launched from a mobile transporter, like a huge articulated truck. Despite the Special Forces steaming around the desert, most of these were never found, and they operated successfully throughout the war.

The Scud might have used old technology, but with a range of one hundred and fifty miles and a one-ton explosive warhead, it had the capacity to do a lot of damage. Being inaccurate, the Iraqis found it difficult to aim them at the troops up at the front. So Saddam kindly gave them to the coffin-dodgers in the rear like myself. The Israelis were also fired on; Saddam hoped to bring them into the war and fracture the coalition, which included Arab forces.

The Iraqis had another clever little trick. They would fly a jet fighter directly upwards on a high trajectory. This looked the same as a Scud on radar, and would set off our air raid procedures. Whether a Scud or not, the standard operating procedure was the same. A raucous alarm would sound out over the tannoy, followed by "Red, Red, Red, Missile Warning Red!"

When the alarm went, we immediately put on respirators, in case there was nerve gas. The protective suit, rubber gloves, and overboots all went on, followed by the Kevlar helmet. Then there was a mad dash to one of the bomb shelters. The shelter's exterior wall consisted of a double layer of oil drums filled with sand. The roof was covered with steel plates and layers of sandbags. Some people found being in them reassuring, and some didn't. I wasn't too bothered either way, though I preferred to keep near the exit, as they felt a bit like graves.

We still didn't have any Allied casualties coming into the hospital. So there wasn't much to do, apart from training. A lot of people started getting bored, but I found plenty of things with which to occupy myself. Ironically, all the bored people were left doing nothing, and I was put on night duty, looking after the handful of routine sick, plus one postoperative appendicitis patient.

Shortly after I finished my night duty, the group captain in command of the airfield put out orders for a 2300 curfew. This wasn't popular, as it stopped us travelling off to find somewhere to drink. As usual, I was the one to open his mouth. I went to a meeting with the CO to argue for my colleagues, much like a trade union official in a factory would. (Incidentally, only in a medical unit would such a thing be likely to happen.) The CO, to his everlasting credit, listened, and then stuck his neck out by arguing the case to the group captain at the air base.

Eventually, the curfew was lifted for medical staff, which was good for morale. Spirits tended to go up and down. Some people were worried, and some believed the propaganda that everything would be absolutely wonderful. As for me, I admit to feeling a bit tense now and then. If I were the type, I'd have prayed for a peaceful victory. I wasn't the type, however, so I generally got rat-arsed instead.

S., the medical assistant I'd taken up with, and I had parted company. It wasn't very amicable. Looking back, I wish I'd been more understanding. Events later showed she should never have been deployed to a war zone; she cracked up during an air raid.

It was coming to the middle of January, and we were getting quite a few air raid alarms, which often had their funny moments. One night, we had come off night duty, returned to the complex, and gone to bed. At about 1000 hours, "Gas, Gas, Gas!" came over the tannoy. Everyone leapt out of bed and donned respirators. I thought it would be a good time to get my will signed, which had arrived by post the previous night.

There were seven of us sat around the room in respirators in varying degrees of dress. I looked over at my pal Stuart.

"Stu, do you think this is the war really starting?" I asked.

He shrugged and muttered through his gas mask, "Fucked if I know."

Tim was struggling to get on his NBC protective overboots. He paused for a second. "What's got into your head?" he asked.

Then, with a flourish, I pulled out some sheets of A4 paper from an envelope.

"Lads," I said, "Will you witness my will, just in case we get blown up?"

Tim and Stu both signed my will, and we looked at each other for a brief moment of sombre silence. Then the laughter started.

However, the really funny bit is what the girls told us later. It seems S. really flipped during the air raid. She ran around their room wearing her respirator, the top half of her NBC protective suit, and silky pyjama bottoms. She was clutching a Bible in her left hand and an atropine injector, or combo pen, in the right.

"I'm feeling twitchy!" she shouted, thinking she had nerve gas poisoning, and tried to inject herself with the atropine injector. The other girls restrained her until the all-clear sounded, by which time she had calmed down. When I was told, I almost pissed myself laughing. I would have loved to watch it happening. As it turned out, it was all a false alarm; someone had fired a Bofors gun, and the alarm stemmed from that.

Chapter Nineteen

Life continued, full of surreal moments and odd contradictions. At the hospital, it was all air raid shelter, helmet, and individual protective equipment (IPE). But at the complex, there wasn't an air raid shelter or even any tape on the windows, and in my room we couldn't hear the tannoy. One day, the alarm sounded and the first thing I knew about it was dimly hearing the all-clear.

One moment we were being told to take NAPS tablets, which are only taken when chemical attack is imminent. The next moment people were being told that NBC kit was available and would be issued "if it was needed."

Some of the girls didn't have a spare NBC suit or spare filters for their respirators. Imagine sitting in a biologically or chemically contaminated environment and not being able to change the filter on your gas mask. I'd have gone ballistic if someone told me I couldn't have a spare canister. I had plenty of spare NBC suits, plus two spare respirator filters. It all got sorted out eventually, but it was just as well that there wasn't an immediate NBC attack.

In the meantime, my sister wrote to me with the news from home. It seemed that angry citizens had smashed some immigrant taxi drivers' windows. Displaying pictures of Saddam in Doncaster wasn't the brightest thing to do. She also told me that the weather wasn't too great.

It wasn't exactly bright where I was, either. We'd had two days of torrential rain, and the hospital was half flooded. The locals thought we were loonies to put it where it was as, apparently, it always floods there.

But the weather wasn't my biggest concern. It was January 16, and the deadline for the withdrawal of Iraqi troops had expired the day before. There was no sign of any Iraqi troop movements, and people were getting a bit tense and twitchy. The worst bit was not knowing what would happen or when.

We were doing twelve-hour shifts by now, and I was on the night shift. To keep us occupied, we had plenty of air raid practices and spent some time in the shelters. Luckily, the shelters were above ground; the water table was only three feet below us, and if they'd have been dug below, they'd have flooded. But, lacking any casualties, we slept from midnight till 0600.

It was just as well we didn't have any casualties. The hospital was in a bad way, and I didn't think we'd cope very well; there didn't seem to be enough basic equipment, such as bandages, dressings, drugs, IV fluids, etc.

Regardless of our state of preparedness, the situation was about to change dramatically. The final deadline for the Iraqis to withdraw their troops expired, and the air war commenced at 0200 on January 17.

The Iraqis had a substantial air force. But by now, the Allied forces were immense, with over twenty five hundred aircraft in the Gulf, giving us overwhelming air superiority. Saddam mostly kept his aircraft hidden away in (supposedly) bombproof shelters and didn't put them up against our lads. We used precision weapons to destroy Iraqi aircraft inside the shelters. Eventually, Saddam sent the remainder to safety in Iran, where they sat out the rest of the war, to the delight of the Iraqi pilots who were spared martyrdom on his behalf.

By the end of the war, the RAF flew over six thousand missions. I watched, devoid of sympathy for the Iraqis, as the Tornados and Jaguars took off to bomb their forward positions and rear echelon infrastructure. I was totally behind the concept of bombing them to help reduce our own force's casualties - not that I recall Stormin' Norman Schwarzkopf asking me.

My two best mates, Tim and Stuart, shared my enthusiasm for bombing the Iraqis into the next world. We were keen to do our jobs and prepared for whatever was to come. But we also shared a concern about the lack of weapons with which to defend ourselves and debated the best course of action to take if things went wrong. As medics, it was our duty to stay with the wounded. But what if we didn't have any wounded and the Iraqis headed south and broke through our frontline defences? If we had weapons to fight with, we were prepared to do just that. We couldn't see why we should sit around defenceless, waiting to be captured.

So we bought shemaghs and bits and pieces of Arab dress in case we needed to disguise ourselves. We spent time travelling around doing little recces, or reconnaissance, to see where there were vehicles or any means of escape. As time went on, it became clear that the chances of the Iraqis breaking through anywhere had gone, so our escape and evasion plans turned into a bit of a joke, but it was serious enough when we started.

Sometime late on the evening of January 16, we were all called to a briefing. The CO stood up and told us that talks between James Baker and Tariq Aziz had failed, and the UN deadline for the removal of Iraqi troops from Kuwait had now expired. The inference was clear: things were going to get bloody - but at least something was going to happen. After the briefing, most of us went off to get some kip.

At about 0245 on January 17, one of the sergeants woke us. The CO gave a briefing and told us the first strike had gone in, a strike to knock out Iraqi air defence radars. For me, it was a relief that the waiting and uncertainty were over. Others had mixed emotions: some of the girls were crying and some were quite lighthearted.

We were sent into the Colpro. We sat and relaxed - but not for long. The tannoy went "Red, Red, Red!" which meant five minutes warning of an air raid. We all sat there in our gas masks, waiting. A female officer said we should lie under the beds. "Be a lot better off in the air raid shelter," I said. But the officer was unsure, so we continued to lie there. The tension was palpable. What was coming next - bombs, explosions? I told a few lame jokes, which got a couple of respirator-muffled laughs. But nothing happened, and then the all-clear sounded.

Whilst the pilots were busy bombing the Iraqis back into the last century, I carried on my more mundane tasks at the hospital. Guard duty was often good for a few laughs. One evening when on guard at the hospital entrance, I had a soldier from the Bahrain Defence Force with me. He was Jordanian, andhe seemed a nice enough chap.

We sat by the side of the road and chatted in a mixture of Arabic and English. It wasn't exactly sophisticated communication. He looked at me and said, "Thatcher sheet."

What's this nutter on about? I thought. "What?"

He tried again. "Thatcher - ees - sheet."

It came to me then. "Ah, you mean Thatcher is shit?"

He nodded.

"Thatcher good - Saddam shit," I replied.

"No, no, Saddam strong," he said, raising his arm and fist in a gesture that made it clear where he thought Saddam's strength lay.

Then the air raid alarm sounded. We both ran to the sandbag sangar (shelter) at the side of the road. The Jordanian, in his haste, left his M16 rifle behind. Clearly reluctant to leave the shelter of the sandbags, he looked at me.

"Pleez, you get my rifle," he implored. I had to laugh at his cheek, but no doubt my answer isn't difficult to guess.

Several days later, one of the bandsmen came down with appendicitis, so one of our doctors removed it in the operating theatre. This was the RAF's first ever operation inside Colpro, and I was the first RAF nurse to look after a postoperative patient inside one. An historic moment that I could have done without, being keen to get some kip

When I got off duty, I'd only been asleep for an hour when the Tannoy blared, "Red, Red, Red!" I leapt out of bed, put on my respirator, and switched on the radio to Radio Bahrain, which was how we kept up with what was going on. An Arab newsreader tried hard to sound dispassionate: "There are reports coming in of missiles landing in Tel Aviv."

Whenever missiles were fired, the whole area went on alert until it was known where they were aimed. It was a relief to hear of them going to someone else, although not much fun for the Israelis.

By then, air activity was getting intense and we were beginning to lose air crew. Two guys, a pilot and a navigator, who came down in Iraq were recovered by the SAS, but then we heard another of our crews had been killed. With the war escalating, we were ordered to take nerve agent pre-treatment sets (NAPS tablets). I felt that this was overdoing things, but the brass was flapping about the mobile Scuds. As an alternative to the one ton of conventional explosives, Scuds could also carry chemical weapons. There was a lot of fuss in the press about this. I blithely wrote home, reassuring my family that chemicals weren't being used, though I've since discovered that they actually were.

Every day we were briefed with the latest war news. The news on January 23, 1991, was bad. The story of the SAS rescue of the two ejected aircrew turned out to be bullshit. They had been captured and tortured by the Iraqis; it was pretty obvious now that their battered faces were plastered over the world's television screens.

Lacking casualties ourselves, someone made the sensible decision to stop the twelve-hour day and night shifts. Instead, we did two shifts during the day. But whatever one shift did, the other shift undid immediately afterwards.

The air activity continued to intensify, and the roar of aircraft taking off to bomb the Iraqis seemed unrelenting. Life had a surreal feeling to it. During the day, at the hospital, it was all Kevlar helmets and respirators. Then, in the evening, it was civvies and socialising in the bar. At times, I felt bad about not taking a more active part in the war. But I'd chosen to join the RAF nursing service, and I was duty bound in wartime to get on with it and do my best for them, which is what I did.

Through it all, television coverage was unrelenting. Journalists and camera crews appeared every few days. Most of us posed heroically as requested, though on one occasion it caused some temporary bother. The CO called us for one of his impromptu briefings.

"Guys, the prime minister has seen us on the television. He's concerned that we weren't wearing Red Cross armbands. So wear them, as the Geneva Convention requires us to do so," the CO commanded.

We all obliged for a couple of days and then went back to normal. I couldn't help reflecting that the prime minister must have had too much spare time on his hands if he could worry about such trivia. Perhaps the IRA thought the same, because they launched a mortar attack on 10 Downing Street around this time. It wasn't very successful and no one was injured. I was glad to hear this, though I only gave it passing thought, being more concerned with getting ready to do guard duty later that day.

Being a believer in good security, I was happy to do my bit on guard. But I bitterly resented the times I was unarmed. We worked in pairs, one of us armed and one not, the person with a weapon chosen by administrative whim.

I couldn't see the logic of having unarmed sentries in a war zone. Maybe it was down to the weapon-hating attitude of some senior nursing staff who, with respect to military matters, had their heads up their arses, ignoring the reality of war. Guard duty did have its lighter moments, though. I used to chat with the Arab soldiers and learnt how to say "fuck off" in Arabic, plus a few other more social phrases that I can no longer remember.

The CO came round and gave a briefing during the night. After passing on the latest war news, he decided to finish with a couple of jokes. To give him his due, he made a good job of it. He stood up on the side of a concrete blast wall and told us to come closer in his best “Monty addressing the troops” style.

“Right, lads - regrettably, we’ve been informed that the Irish government has broken the trade embargo,” he revealed.

This got everyone’s attention, as he no doubt expected. “Yes, they’ve sold a new kind of missile to the Iraqis; it’s called the Spud.”

A good-natured groan went up from the crowd. Emboldened, he carried on. “Also, it’s been reported on the news that the Irish government is sending troops to the Gulf.” He paused for effect. “The Mexican government is wondering what to do with them!”

Hours later, I sat writing to my sister. It must have been about four in the morning. As usual, the night sky was beautifully still and clear. I sat on a casualty stretcher, gazing up at the mass of twinkling stars. Then the roar of a jet fighter landing across the road broke my reverie. Back in reality, I took a sip from my mug of tea and got on with the letter. I told her about the new sleeping bags with which we'd all been issued. They came with a gore-tex bivvy bag, a waterproof breathable fabric sleeping bag cover, used as a lightweight substitute for a tent. These were expensive items and meant to be handed back in, but I saw an opportunity. I went around buying them for ten pounds each and then sent them home in a box to my sister, who sold them at a profit on my behalf to members of the Territorial Army. On a less mercenary note, I also sent letters to my nieces Jennifer and Danielle. Pam told me that they were upset watching the television coverage of the war, and I remember feeling sad and thinking that Saddam had a lot to answer for.

Indeed, Saddam had plenty to trouble his conscience. We'd been told that the injuries on the faces of the captured pilots probably happened ejecting from their Tornado after being hit by Iraqi fire.

Their faces were plastered all over the world's television screens, and much later we discovered how badly the Iraqis had tortured these poor guys. Being located so close to the airfield, we often saw the pilots, and everyone felt their loss in a quite personal way.

One of the pilots who was later shot down (his navigator was killed) was called Rupert. I remember standing behind him in the dinner queue. His name was written on his flying suit, and I made some limp joke to my mate about it being appropriate, since officers in the forces were nicknamed 'ruperts'. Of course, it wasn't said with any malice. The pilots were all very brave men who deserve our respect and gratitude.

By the end of January, most of us had stopped taking the NAPS tablets, as we were unhappy about the side effects. Then I was told we were to be vaccinated against the plague; I didn't know whether to laugh or cry. If I was the crying type, there was plenty to cry about. Our bombers roared off from the runway in a constant stream, killing Iraqis on a daily basis. Massive oil slicks drifted down the Gulf, leaving a trail of oil-drenched seabirds. The Iraqis were systematically and comprehensively looting Kuwait. Rumour had it that we were to be shifted up to the front. The emphasis of our intelligence briefings shifted from, "It'll be over soon," to the prospect of a long and bloody war.

But I wasn't the crying type. Rather, I tried to find the humour in it all, especially the NAPS tablets. Some of the lads had been getting short-term side effects of stomach and bowel upsets, disturbed sleep, and intense weird dreams. One of the lads actually jumped up whilst dreaming and head-butted the bunk above him. It caused a good laugh. But nonetheless, everyone gradually stopped taking them.

But we didn't know then that NAPS were pyrodistigmine bromide. This powerful drug has potentially severe side effects on the central nervous system, and had not been tested on humans for its current use. Of course, if we had known that, we'd have stopped even quicker.

By the beginning of February, we'd been in the Gulf for five weeks, getting the unit ready to receive casualties. Then, when I went into the tented hospital, I found them shifting and rearranging the beds yet again. I had a mega sense-of-humour failure and went and sat inside the cool and calm of an air raid shelter.

When I got back to the accommodation later that afternoon, I told Stuart about the latest frenzy of reorganisation on at the "Carry On War Hospital." We had a laugh about it, and I regained my usual composure.

Later, Tim Hill read a letter from his auntie. It was brilliant. Tim held out the bluey and read out loud, with his usual grin and his eyes twinkling above his slightly tatty moustache: "We watch CNN News on the TV, it's on twenty-four hours a day and they keep filling it with repeats of the Gulf - it must be really boring out there for you." That brought a few laughs.

Not to be outdone, Stuart added some news. "Have you heard about Colin, one of the RAF Reserve chaps who's just arrived? He's a British rock-and-roll dancing champ - been on

Come Dancing on TV and so on - he's started Lambada classes here." Then Stu struck a heroic pose and said, "It's a man's life in the RAF!"

In addition to the RAF Reserve unit, we also inherited half a dozen medics from the Dutch Navy, plus around twenty from the Royal New Zealand Navy. I got on very well with the Kiwis, especially a lad called Dave, with whom I shared more than a few beers.

We were also blessed with regular visits from the media. The ITN news crew was especially entrepreneurial. They took bits of newsreel and outtakes and made up a one-hour video, which they sold in quantity to the hospital. It was our airfield, our planes, and our pilots, and some of the pilots on the video were dead by then, so it was very personal to Muharraq. Nonetheless, humour always surfaces; one of my favourite bits is a Tornado pilot climbing out of the cockpit after a raid over Iraq, waving a bag of urine at the camera crew.

It was about this time that Tim came up to me with the latest buzz.

“Hey, Bob," he said one day. "There’s a rumour that we may be getting some Iraqi POWs tonight.”

I remember my reply. “I hope it’s just a rumour, because I’d personally rather let the bastards bleed to death - though our lot will probably have a whip round and take them on as lifelong pen pals.” They were never sent to us, but we did get some new kit, which was much more welcome.

Around the same time, the RAF finally issued us with desert combat uniforms. Due to some strange error on the RAF’s part, mine fitted perfectly. Of course, the RAF won in the end, because as soon as I washed them, the trousers shrunk, and I could barely get them on.

To add to my joy, we had a visit the same day from the commander of medical services (CMS). As always, I had something to say - the lads expected it by then. I asked about the likelihood of casualties coming to us, and the CMS gave a noncommittal reply, which I can't remember now. But the feeling I got, reading between the lines, was that our hospital wasn't considered to be much, and we wouldn't be doing much, unlike the hospitals nearer the front.

The day after the CMS blessed us with a visit, on February 7, I decided to kill some time by standing on the roof, photographing the bombers taking off. They were too far away, though, so I went down the road next to the runway. This felt close enough to wish the pilots good luck as they whizzed past. But being there brought predictable results.

As I raised my telephoto lens in the direction of a jet exhaust, an Arab policeman appeared, clutching a pistol, looking decidedly suspicious. Eventually, my RAF ID card and many repetitions of "*salaam alaikum*" (an Arabic greeting meaning "God be with you") placated him, and I legged it before he could get some backup.

My next photographic foray was to the fire station. They had a tower that I wanted to climb, but the Arab Fire Chief insisted on sending me up on a massive turntable ladder. An Arab fireman raised himself and me on the ladder's platform until we reached a little opening on the outside of the tower. This was where things got a little shaky.

He struggled with the fine adjustments of the hydraulic controls, and the ladder lurched backwards and forwards. The gap between the ladder and the tower opened and closed, whilst the fireman smiled with look of embarrassment. Seeing my chance, I jumped the gap and landed in the tower opening. I shouted my thanks whilst promising myself a descent via the metal rungs on the tower wall. I got some great photos.

The following day, February 8, I decided to take a stroll to the airfield. Once there, I persuaded one of the technicians to let me sit in the pilot's seat of a Tornado fighter. I acted like a twelve-year-old, and I had to laugh at myself.

Later that afternoon, two Kuwaiti interpreters joined the hospital. They weren't professional soldiers. They were just civvies who were fortunate to be out of their country when the Iraqis invaded. Their attitude toward the Iraqis was predictably venomous;

they were very, very happy that bombs were being dropped on the Iraqi Army.

They were less happy about the Scud alerts which we had during the next few nights, though the rest of us were getting used to them. After one particularly disturbed night though, I decided to go over on the following morning and write some obnoxious messages on the bombs. I sent regards on behalf of family and friends, and then took a photograph to send to them.

I enjoyed photography, and one of my photos was published in the RAF nursing magazine. One of the officers was a really good photographer, and she actually sold her photographs. I think she also won the competition to design a RAFWH unit badge. The winning design featured a red cross with a palm tree over a blue (RAF) background. I thought it a good idea to have an alternative version. My design was an oval-shaped badge, with a palm tree in the centre, the hospital's location, "Muharraq", underneath, and

"R.O.M.F.T" (a commonly heard Navy acronym meaning "roll on my fucking time") above.

I got an Arab tailor to make some of my badges on khaki cloth. Tim Hill, Stu Leverton and a few of the lads and I sewed them on our desert camouflageshirts. This was totally unofficial, of course, and against all regulations, but no one seemed to mind. A few of the officers even started to wear them, though I doubt they realised the meaning of the initials.

Lots of us killed time by visiting the airfield to take photographs. On some occasions it was officially sanctioned, and sometimes it wasn't. I think the authorities genuinely didn't want to stop our budding David Baileys from keeping themselves busy. But at the same time, they were concerned about pictures of the airfield and sensitive kit like the laser-guided bombs getting into the hands of Arab developing shops. Fearing pictures might end up heading to Iraqi intelligence sources, unofficial photography was eventually banned.

That day, I stood chatting with an official photographer, who told me he was taking photos for a museum. After he left, I decided to quietly continue walking around taking pictures of the nose art on the aeroplanes.

An armed guard standing by one of the fighters asked me what I was doing.

"I'm taking pictures for the museum," I replied.

"What museum?" he asked suspiciously.

What fucking museum? I thought, having no idea who the real photographer had been working for.

Luckily for me, the second armed guard misinterpreted my look of horror. He must have imagined I was staring at his mate, thinking him an idiot. So he interjected, "RAF Museum, of course."

"Of course," I said, with a big inward sigh of relief, and continued taking photos.

Soon after this, on February 18, we had a visit from Air Chief Marshall (ACM) Sir Patrick Hine, the joint British Field Force commander. A selected number of yes-men (and women) were nominated to meet the great man. By now I was known to be a little outspoken—I'd bent the ears of all the other dignitaries and senior people sent to visit or brief us. So it was no surprise to find myself excluded.

However, a junior officer and a SNCO sabotaged the list. The CO arrived on the ward with the ACM and his entourage. He gave a look of horror when he saw me. Then the ACM moved in my direction, but the CO moved with the grace and speed of a ballet dancer, putting his six-foot-plus bulk between me and the ACM and his bodyguards. I suppose the CO wasn't going to take any chances - you can't really blame him. Even if I didn't always see eye to eye with him, I couldn't help respecting him more and more as time went on.

Chapter Twenty

In mid-February, a little good news came our way at the morning briefing: the CO announced that we weren't being charged for food and accommodation. This was backdated to when the war started. The bad news was that some bloody civil servant from the Ministry of Defence in London had been out to see if they could change the rationing system. The aim was to enable the RAF to give us all meals and then take away the one hundred and thirty pounds per week we were getting as ration money. It was an irony of the rationing system though that we ended up being paid at a higher rate in our comfy billets than the troops farther up at the front.

Later that day, I went across to the post to send some things home to my sister. I included some military maps, to which I attached a little note: "I've obtained some maps of Baghdad for you. However, certain features, such as Grid 4290, MOD, and Iraqi Army HQ, no longer exist."

Though we knew elements of the Iraqi forces were being bombed out of existence, it was obvious that there was soon going to be a big, bloody land battle. But we continued with the minutiae of life. I moved the focus of my activities from photography to getting fit. I'd rashly entered for the Bahrain International Marathon to be held on Friday, February 22· I knew that some people were waiting for me to fall on my face, but I determined to show them differently. With only five days to prepare, I knew I was pushing my luck.

A couple of days before the race, I was sat in the canteen tent set up in the centre of the hospital complex that a couple of Arabs, who appeared from somewhere or other, ran. They fixed up a television, which I watched occasionally.

I sat casually, watching CNN. They were showing a live interview with a young US Marine Corps lance corporal who had been wounded at Khafji. His armoured personnel carrier (APC) had been hit by what they thought was probably friendly fire, and all his section - seven men - were killed, except for him. The bloody stupid bastard reporter asked him idiot questions: did he feel guilty for surviving, and was he angry? I can't remember the corporal's exact reply, but he answered with great dignity and modesty. Then they proceeded with a live phone-in from the USA.

A woman whose husband was killed at Khafji phoned. She asked the lance corporal if he had known her husband. He said, "Yes, your husband died in my APC." (No doubt the CNN newsmen knew this beforehand.)

She asked, "Did my husband see the photos I sent?"

He said they'd seen each other's photos, and that her husband "had been a great guy and a real hero."

"God bless you," she said, and told him how glad she was that he was still alive and to please get in touch with her.

It was all stiff upper lip stuff. They were both so brave and dignified. I had a lump in my throat and had to leave the tent. If I'd watched any more, I'd have been in tears.

On the night before the marathon, I sat on the sandbag entrance to an air raid shelter and looked up at the stars again. I wondered how I'd do. Compared to that marine, my concerns about running my first marathon were paltry. But unless the war escalated in the next few hours, I'd be there. I was the only one from RAFWH running the full marathon; the rest were doing the half. I didn't give a damn what my time was, so long as I finished. Then I made myself a promise that I'd finish if it bloody killed me. Just then, Flight Sergeant John Wilson came up to shake my hand and wish me luck. He was a real gent.

The race started at 0600, and I got off to a good start whilst it was still cool. A few of our guys passed by and shouted some words of encouragement. I was happy to let them go; I had twice the distance to run and needed to pace myself. As I ran, I thought about the race - and my own military career.

I knew that I wasn't a great athlete, just like I knew that I wasn't ever going to be some tough Special Forces type. I'd chopped and changed and never shown the commitment needed to realise my full potential in the military. But in my own little way, I'd served my country, and at least I'd stayed in the race. With that thought in mind, I determined to do my best, and whilst I didn't win the marathon, I at least made it to the end.

I took twenty-fourth place in the Bahrain International Marathon with a time of three hours, fifty-nine minutes, and thirty-six seconds. Not bad at all - though, of course, all the real athletes had ‘chickened out’ of running because of the war.

The first Gulf War, fought to liberate Kuwait, was massively popular with the public, and reported on to the nth detail in the UK press. All sorts of human interest stories appeared. Later, in March, an article appeared in the *Doncaster Courier*: “Medic on the Run in the Gulf.” There was a photograph of me with the caption, “More worried about the marathon than Scud missiles!” They quoted me as saying, “Considering I had only been training for the marathon for five days and had very little sleep the night before, due to pre-race nerves and two Scud missile attacks, I was very pleased with my result.” But of course there were far more important things about to happen, as I soon found out.

Two days after the marathon, on the February 24, we were woken at about 0400 by another missile attack. We later found out it was aimed at Saudi Arabia. It also coincided with the start of the ground war—the shit had really hit the fan. We were called together for a briefing and told that the first wave of troops was going in and that we could expect casualties. (The Army's original estimate was fifteen percent, though I'd heard all sorts of estimates bandied about since then). As always, emotions varied, but in general people were taking it in their stride; after all, that's what we were there for.

Naturally, as a field hospital expecting casualties, we had a priest on the strength. One of the girls spoke up: "Padre, do you think we should say a prayer?" Then he obliged with a "Lord protect us all through the forthcoming death and misery" prayer. By the time he finished, half the girls were in tears and - in my opinion - morale had plummeted. But my morale remained constant, and when the shift finished I went off and slept.

The following evening, I walked into the hospital at 1730. The Colpro and the main ward had more or less been abandoned. Everything was being totally reorganised into a unit next door that had been emptied that day. So after sitting on our backsides for the last thirty days, here we were, reorganising and starting again from scratch, and this with the ground attack going on and (we thought) mass casualties on the way. I cannot print my comments here.

Fortunately, the Allied casualty rate was extremely low. It became apparent that it was likely to stay that way, and I increasingly sensed that what casualties there were would go to the big hospitals at Dhahran and Al Jubayl, and be evacuated by air from there.

Sometimes I'd watch various units going off to the front, and it made me feel as guilty as hell to be doing so little for much of the time. I had a word with some RAF Regiment officers, asking about units that might be short of a medic and expressed a willingness to join them. It didn't come to anything but probably made me feel a little better about things.

I did move within the hospital though, from the wards to the preoperative area. I was happy with this, as there were some good people there. One officer, Debbie, came from near Doncaster, where my family lived. The sergeant, Bob Sanderson, was a good guy, too, and we got on well.

The evening of my move was livened up by an air raid and a dash for the shelters. Some of the lads had stopped bothering to put on their NBC kit and respirators. It was too much trouble, and the all-clear generally sounded by the time they were finished donning the gear. They seemed to think that because we hadn't been hit yet, it would never happen. But I continued to play it by the book, and my NBC drills got slicker and slicker.

At about 0200, the alarm sounded "Red, Red, Red!" again. I legged it to an air raid shelter. One of the lads ran in and shouted, "Hey Bob! What's the new Saudi national anthem?"

"Dunno - what?" I answered.

"Onwards, Christian soldiers!" he said, putting on his respirator as he should have done immediately upon hearing the alarm. When the all-clear sounded, I got a stretcher and kipped outside, enjoying a pleasant night under the stars. Later that morning, we discovered the alarm was caused by a Scud missile that killed twenty-one Americans and injured another ninety.

Chapter Twenty-One

After what was one of the shortest ground wars in history (it lasted one hundred hours), the Iraqis surrendered. The ceasefire was announced to us at 0800 on February 28, 1991.

The bar immediately opened, and a good deal of celebration commenced. The beer flowed and everyone laughed and joked.

Of course, the Iraqis weren't celebrating. I felt quite sorry for them, but thinking about the poor Kuwaitis tended to reduce my sympathy dramatically.

Once the initial euphoria died down, one burning question occupied everyone's mind: *When are we going home?* As yet, no one really knew. We were told that Prime Minister Major wanted to "bring the boys back home" - and he also wanted the boys up at the sharp end to go first (and rightly so).

We had another briefing. The CO warned us that we would probably be the last hospital to leave, saying "So long as the

Commander British Forces Middle East feels there's a need for a Brit hospital in the Gulf, we are staying. Anyway, we won't go until the Tornado and Jaguar squadrons across the road go."

Then, he wisely hedged his bets: "However, things are changing from day to day, so . . ."

Naturally, it was a great relief that the war was over. It was good to go to sleep at night knowing the air raid alarm wouldn't wake us. We didn't have to carry respirators, and for the first few days it felt a bit strange. I kept getting momentary panic attacks, thinking I'd lost the bloody thing. Then I'd remember that I didn't have to carry it.

The hospital warrant officer, a really nice chap, called me in one morning. He was a runner, and I got on well with him.

He said, "Bob, there's a fifty-mile desert relay race on the fifteenth, an Ultra-Marathon. Someone at the airfield has come up with the idea of entering someone to run the full fifty miles—a special entry to do a big sponsorship thing for charity. They asked if we have anyone likely to have a go?" Then he looked at me in a kindly sort of way. "I told them that we've only got one person crazy enough to try that."

After all that, I could hardly say no, but I couldn't help thinking it was going to be one hell of a personal challenge.

Shortly after this, I heard that we might be getting Iraqi wounded at RAFWH, so I went to the hospital to check out what was going on. I discovered that the bit about the Iraqi wounded was just a rumour. I also discovered that I was rostered for all-night guard duty on the fourteenth, and the race was on the fifteenth. I couldn't believe it; some dork thought I was going to stay up all night on sodding guard and then go straight out and run fifty miles.

I looked at an admin clerk and politely enquired, "Are there any more tasks for me, such as walking on water or raising the dead?"

In reality, there was no need for my sarcasm. The guard duty was an oversight, and I had it cancelled with no problem at all.

In the absence of any firm news, we happily debated whatever rumours turned up. Arab radio stations were a potent source of information and gossip—and sometimes it was quite accurate, too. There were cryptic remarks on the radio about how much the emir of Bahrain loved British troops and how much he thanked Tom King for our help. In the meantime, the 'planes were still sat next door, fully bombed up and awaiting the signing of a formal ceasefire.

On March 8, rumour was replaced by reality. 4626 Aeromedical Evacuation Squadron (the reserve unit that brought us Colin the dancing medic) was told to pack up and be ready to go home the next day. The Dutch medics attached to us were told they were leaving, too. Then Dave, my friend from the Kiwi Navy, came to see me. He told me that their guys were leaving on the eighteenth.

The hospital looked like an ant nest that had been poked with a big stick. People were running around like headless chickens, taking down tents and returning stores. I decided I could best help the situation by demonstrating an aura of calm, so I went off to the canteen tent to read the newspaper and drink tea.

Later in the day, I went out to prepare for the race. The weather was strange. The wind was blowing from the northwest, and I could taste oil in it as I ran, breathing hard. There was a horrid black tinge in the sky, too, the result of the burning Kuwaiti oilfields.

The subject of Iraqi casualties figured prominently in the press back home. Initially, we heard reports of one hundred thousand dead. Then we heard that it could be nearer to two hundred thousand. But, of course, it was only speculation. Even now, I doubt if there are any accurate casualty figures.

But that's the reality of war - men die. I make no apology for being glad that the Iraqis, and not our lads, paid the overwhelming bulk of the butcher's bill. Anyway, by comparison to our Kuwaiti interpreters, I looked like a washy-washy liberal. Having seen the Iraqi army march into Kuwait and loot, murder, and rape their merry way through their country, the Kuwaitis would have happily carried on the war until Iraq was a smoking ruin. But the clear and universally agreed-upon aim of liberating Kuwait had been achieved, and I was truly glad it was over.

You probably think that the war was just about oil, but that wasn't how those of us who took part saw it. We were there because it was our job to implement the policies of the government, the government that the people voted into office. We went because it was our duty to do so. Many of us even volunteered, afraid that we wouldn't be sent. The average serviceman didn't think about oil, but did have a lot of sympathy for the Kuwaitis and thought it right and proper to give the Iraqis a kick up the arse.

But you can't take oil out of it. What if Iraq had been left with the Kuwaiti oilfields and then gone on to push a little further into Saudi Arabia and Bahrain? Saddam would have been left in control of half the world's oil reserves. Would you really want that sort of power in the hands of a vicious butcher from the same psychological mould as Hitler or Stalin?

Think how easy it would have been to cut off the oil supplies and watch the western democracies slide into petrol rationing, economic chaos, and another three-day week - followed by massive unemployment and a slide into the living standards of the third world. So, politically, it was about oil, too. But to the average serviceman, it was about doing the right thing and standing up for the rights of a small nation in the clutches of an extremely unpleasant dictator. I couldn't help dwelling on all this as I ran mile after mile in preparation for the race. It was easy to get fanciful. Was the hint of oil in the air more than just a reminder of recent events? Was it also a portent of things to come?

I was glad when the day of the race, March 15, arrived. Because of the heat, the organisers of the race started it early, at 0600. The CO got hold of a civvy car as a backup vehicle, and Tim Hill and another lad were there to drive around behind me with supplies of water. The relay teams started a little later than the five of us who were running the whole fifty miles, which gave us a clear start. We set off, and I went into the lead, wanting to make as much progress as I could whilst it was still cool. It felt great to be out running, despite that persistent tinge in the air of burning oil. A little later, the shift started back at the hospital, and I was told they listened as the race was reported on the radio, following my progress. Paul Sexby, an Army signaller, passed me, and that was the last I saw of him. He was an accomplished athlete, having previously taken part in two hundred-mile races, and I had no illusions about beating him.

A couple of U.S. Marines from the embassy were also running. We ran together for quite some time until we eventually parted with a handshake as they went on ahead. There must have been some crazy psychology involved, because the first twenty-five miles were easy. In effect, I was running two marathons, one straight after the other. I expected to be tired as I finished the first one, but I still felt fresh and ready for more.

But if the first one was easy, the second was one of the toughest things I've ever done. After about thirty miles, my muscles ached and my body screamed for rest. Tim and the other lad were great. They appeared at just the right time with supplies of water and words of support and encouragement.

After about forty miles, I was well and truly knackered. Every muscle screamed for rest, and I pondered my sanity in having agreed to do this. It was more like speed marching now—run a little, then walk a little. The faster relay teams, swapping over from the back of support vehicles, had passed by and finished long ago. It was just me left.

The CO and Warrant Officer Hugh Bairnfather (sorry if I've spelt it wrong, Hugh), plus a handful of others, appeared in vehicles. They lined the side of the road, clapping me on, before driving on ahead to do the same again. It was decent of them, but much as I appreciated their support, I was hurting and finding it hard to put on a smile. I asked Tim to politely tell them all to bugger off. They did, though Tim told me that one or two were just a little offended.

Ten hours after setting off, I put on a final burst of speed and ran into a little sports stadium to finish. The CO and one or two others were there to welcome me with a much-appreciated beer. Then it was back to the complex for another beer in the sergeant's mess with John Wilson, followed by a shower (without John Wilson, I hasten to add).

I later discovered that Paul Sexby had won, with a time of seven hours, eight minutes, and forty-one seconds. I'm not sure about the two Marines, except both they and the fourth Ultra-Marathon runner came in before me. The relay teams were in the bar later, and I seem to remember joining some of them for a beer or two. It felt good to have faced up to such a big challenge and to have stuck it out and achieved my goal. It gave me a lot of self confidence and belief in myself. Indeed, perhaps it was instrumental in helping me to face another big challenge later on ... when I left the services and gained Bachelor's and Master's degrees.

But I digress.

After the race, the commander of the RAF detachment in Muharraq, Group Captain Henderson, sent for me. He congratulated me on the run and for the five hundred and seventy-six dinars raised in sponsorship money for the RAF Benevolent Fund. It was decent of the group captain, who was busy sending the fighter squadrons home, to make time for me.

An even bigger surprise was to come. The day before No4 RAFWH was due to return to the UK, the CO called the whole unit together for a talk. He jumped up onto a table and called us all towards him. We all made bleating sheep noises and crowded forward in a mass.

The CO thanked us all for our efforts. Then, to my amazement, he called me forward and told me to stand on the table. He looked at me and said, "When we first met, I thought Bob Widders was an idiot, always beating my ears about having a weapon and wanting to guard us all."

He went on to congratulate me about the first marathon and the fifty-mile Desert Ultra-Marathon.

"I hadn't intended to name a man of the match, but if I did, it would be Bob, the toughest man I've ever met," he said. He then presented me with a specially inscribed unit crest. I was utterly stunned and, for once, quite speechless. It was a special moment, and I'm very grateful to the CO and my comrades from RAFWH.

The following day we flew back to England via Cyprus with RAF Support Command and landed at RAF Lyneham. My sister Pam was there to meet me. We drove straight to RAF Halton, where I sorted out a few quick administrative matters, and then went off on two weeks' leave. It was lovely to get home and see my nieces and sit and talk with my brilliant sister, who'd given me so much love and support through it all. A week or so later, I went down to Bristol and visited old friends, and then it was back to Halton and the usual routine on Ward 6.

Back at Halton, I marked time and looked forward to finishing. I did the Nijmegan March again, but otherwise, boredom and lots of night ward duty prevailed. There was a sort of division between those who'd been deployed in the Gulf and those who hadn't. It was a very quiet and mostly unspoken division, though on one occasion, an operating theatre sister had a sense-of-humour failure and banned all mention of the Gulf in *her* operating theatre. I guess she never went there.

My last night at Halton and in the RAF was far more social than my last night in the Army. I had drinks in the hospital social club with lots of friends, including some of the excellent lads from the RAF Apprentice College, who had been on the Nijmegan March with me. I was glad to go, but a bit sad, too.

Afterword

My years in the Royal Navy shaped my character and moulded me in both positive and negative ways. The Army toughened me and taught me self-reliance and self-discipline. Contrary to popular stereotypes of automata led by screaming and shouting NCOs, at their best, the armed forces function quietly and efficiently, with trained professionals who know their jobs and just get on with it.

I'd gone out to the Gulf full of contempt for the RAF. But by the time the war was over, I had learnt a lot about it and about myself. My letters home had been harsh in their judgments of RAFWH and slow to see the positives, of which there had been many. As events unfolded, I'd gained increasing respect and liking for the CO, Wing Commander Davies. He took on a tough job, for which his real training as a doctor could hardly have prepared him. He'd shown amazing patience and forbearance to me, putting up with insolent questions and suggestions that would have got me in trouble in most outfits.

Regardless of my own boredom at RAF (Hospital) Halton, at least during my service we did have proper military hospitals, where our wounded could receive first-class treatment amongst their comrades in secure dedicated units. Since then, the military hospitals have been closed down in yet more politically-led defence cuts. Now the wounded from Afghanistan and Iraq go to 'military wings', located in civilian hospitals. It saddens me to read in the newspapers that RAF and Army nurses working there have been threatened and abused. It saddens me even more that wounded soldiers have also been subjected to abusive comments by (some) civilians. And it saddens and disgusts me that ungrateful and uncaring politicians have brought this situation about.

Also since the Gulf War, there's been a high incidence of illness amongst Gulf veterans. Lord Lloyd, a former law lord, headed an independent inquiry and found that Gulf veterans are twice as likely to suffer ill health than troops deployed to Bosnia or the UK, for example. The report identifies a number of possible causes. First, there were the multiple vaccine injections, including anthrax and the plague. Then the report cites the indiscriminate spraying of tents with organophosphate pesticides. There was also a low level of exposure to nerve gas, including Sarin, which was originally developed in the 1930s by the Nazis. Finally, there was the inhalation of depleted uranium dust. (Our tanks fired solid depleted uranium shells to destroy enemy tanks, resulting in clouds of uranium-contaminated dust.) Some of those factors have a potentiating effect on each other, made even worse in the presence of stress. And whatever the cause, my own health has deteriorated since the Gulf War with skin and joint problems.

Many ex-servicemen find problems reintegrating into civilian life - I did. Years spent in the armed forces, plus my family's relocation to Devon, resulted in losing touch with childhood friends and the associations and contacts that linked me to my place of origin. I made lots of new mates in the services, but when you leave, they are left behind and you start again. And when the barrack gates finally shut behind you, it can be a lonely world out there. Perhaps this is one reason why a disproportionately large number of homeless males are ex-servicemen.

In fact, up to a quarter of all homeless males sleeping rough on Britain's streets are thought to be ex-servicemen. The military is more than a job - it's an institutionalised lifestyle that often leaves men unprepared to deal with civilian life. After leaving the services, many men feel isolated, missing the camaraderie and support of their fellow soldiers. They experience a sense of alienation in civilian life, worsened by difficulty finding employment. This all adds up to a cycle of despair, and many turn to drink or drugs. Of course, not every ex-serviceman suffers from these problems. I've been luckier than many. Though after serving in - and being discharged from - HM Forces three times, I've experienced enough to understand how bad the problems can be.

Sometimes, in moments of introspection, I wonder what my life would have been like if I'd followed Mother's advice. She wanted me to stay at home, take an apprenticeship, and become a plumber. And perhaps, if I had listened, I'd have been a happier man today, settled in the community with a home and family. But I didn't . . .

So I'll turn to Kipling's poem "*If*", the same poem that stared down at me from the walls of the gymnasium at HMS Ganges on my very first day in the Navy.

If you can fill the unforgiving minute

With sixty seconds' worth of distance run,

Yours is the Earth and everything that's in it,

And - which is more - you'll be a Man, my son.

At least I've filled my life's unforgiving minute to the full. And it's not over yet!

Printed in Great Britain
by Amazon

38100840R00199